MOVE IT

MOVE IT!

An Illustrated History of Heavy Haulage Vehicles at Work

Bob Tuck

PSL

Patrick Stephens
Wellingborough, Northamptonshire

Acknowledgements
The author should like to thank all those who have
given permission for their photographs to be
reproduced in this book. They are, in alphabetical
order: *Bristol Evening Post,* British Petroleum, Central
Electricity Generating Board, *Daily Mail,* John Dyson
FIIP, DGS Films, Ross-shire, General Electric,
Hawker Siddeley, Head Wrightson Teesdale Ltd,
Hendon Times, Lancashire Evening Post, Tom Llewellyn,
N.E.I. Parsons, *Newcastle Chronicle and Journal,*
Peterborough Evening Telegraph, Robert Price, Reflections,
Yarm, *Stafford Newsletter,* Alan Timbrell (British
Airports Authority, Gatwick), Vickers PLC, *Western
Mail and Echo, Wolverhampton Express and Star,* John
Wynn, *Yorkshire Post.*

Others who have helped with research are: John
Banks, Bill Beadnell, Roy Brandley, John Brown, Ted
Fitzpatrick, Paul Hancox, Tom Llewellyn, Eric
Pinchin, Alan Simpson, Peter Sunter, Tim Wayne and
John Wynn. Last but not least are Rick and Dennis
without whose help this book would still be in its
infancy.

Cover illustrations
Front This well turned out Mark 2 Contractor is
hauling a CEGB transformer from Cheshire to
Skelmersdale on 12 July 1984. Seen here near
Ormskirk, the Crane trailer in use is the well-travelled
TM1120, which had a running width of 15 ft, a height
of 15 ft 8 in and an all-up weight of 194 tons.
Back, above Malcolm Johnson is at the helm of
Sunters' Titan II as he eases under Newport Bridge,
Middlesbrough, with one of four 177-tonne vessels
bound for Russia via Hartlepool docks. **Below** Three
of Pickfords' finest leave the main A691 road with a
heavy load for Consett. The Super Constructors had a
five-day haul with this 170-ton roll housing from
Sheffield.

Title page Sunters' first big Contractor close to the
top of Nanny Goat Bank on the A68 between Tow
Law and Castleside in 1970. The Whessoe vehicle built
in Darlington had to criss-cross most of Durham
County due to its dimensions before being delivered to
the steel works at Consett (*Photo Arthur Phillipson*).

First published as *Moving Mountains* and *Mountain
Movers* in 1983 and 1984.
This edition first published in 1987

British Library Cataloguing in Publication Data

Tuck, Bob
    Move it!: an illustrated history of heavy haulage
vehicles at work.
    1. Commercial vehicles—Great Britain—History
I. Title   II. Tuck, Bob. Moving mountains
III. Tuck, Bob. Mountain movers
629.2'24'0941   TL230

    ISBN 1-85260-018-7

*Patrick Stephens is part of the
Thorsons Publishing Group*

Printed and bound in Great Britain

10 9 8 7 6 5 4 3 2 1

Contents

Author's introduction

Of all aspects of road transportation, the field of heavy haulage is arguably the one which has seen the biggest changes over the last two centuries. It was in the 1830s that the steam-powered vehicle became a regular sight on our roads and, in replacing the multi-teamed horses and oxen, the haulier found an ever-increasing potential to move what had previously seemed impossible.

Moving Mountains, the first of the two books combined in this new volume, traces the history of heavy haulage from those pioneering days when wheels were made either of wood or steel and the law required a man to walk in front of the vehicle waving a red flag to warn of its progress. The challenge of moving a 100-ton load was met and overcome in 1929, but in the 1980s the new generation of heavy hauliers are expected to move loads now measured in thousands of tons.

Mountain Movers, the second book, describes the development of those hauling tractors whose common claim is that they are able to haul individual loads of 100 tons or more. The British manufacturer certainly led the world in developing these 100-tonners, but it was to be the Europeans who would throw down the gauntlet, challenge this superiority and so bring about even greater advances in vehicle technology.

Now, *Moving Mountains* and *Mountain Movers* are published together to show in a single volume the strides that man and machine have made in this awe-inspiring field of transport.

BOB TUCK

Left Horse power of the original kind, apparently double headed, seen about to leave John Thompson's at Wolverhampton in the 1890s. The markings on the trailer tend to suggest the outfit was owned by the local railways.

Below Although this photograph was taken in Australia, and as late as 1921, it does show the size and difficulties of the large horse teams which were needed before the introduction of the powerful steam traction engine.

1. In the beginning there was Norman E. Box

The movement of heavy objects from one place to another has been a challenge to man since the beginning of time. The Pyramids and Stonehenge are both famous results of some very heavy hauls, but when it became socially unacceptable to use human slaves, man had to harness the power of the animal to cope with his heaviest load. Even the carriage of goods by barge on the sleepy canals depended on the pulling horse but, with the operation of George Stephenson's most famous invention, the vogue of hundreds of years of transportation was soon to change. 1825 saw *Locomotion* preceded by a man waving a red banner, but the success of the *Rocket* and the Liverpool to Manchester railway in 1829 soon saw the disappearance of the escort, although he did not remain unemployed for long.

In 1801 Richard Trevithick had invented a steam road carriage which could outpace the traditional horse-drawn ones and in 1803 one of his steamers ran in the streets of London. Fellow Cornishman, Sir Goldsworth Gurney, developed this concept and in July 1829 his carriage went from London to Bath and back at a speed of 15 mph. The steam carriage was set to take off but for the political clout which the established stage coach operators and railway owners could muster. Leaders in the commercial field were a well known firm of carters called Pickfords, who had a well organised system similar to a modern day freightliner in operation with the railways carrying their carts nationwide whilst the horses finished the haul from the terminals. To allow the steam wagon in would destroy this business. Legislation created heavy tolls for steam-driven road vehicles and, in 1865, the law enacted a general speed limit for mechanical road vehicles of 4 mph which was further reduced to 2 mph in towns. If this was not oppressive enough, every such vehicle had to be controlled by three persons, one of whom had to walk in front carrying a red flag.

Strangely, the railways failed to take advantage of this virtual monopoly preferring to squabble amongst themselves rather than concentrate on promoting an ideal conception of transport. It took 20 years before a standard gauge was agreed and the 19th century was one continuous conflict between rival companies. Territorial boundaries were closely set and fiercely guarded but had effort been put into making platforms lower, tunnels wider and higher, plus providing more space between opposing lines, then the question asked a century later, 'Why doesn't it go on the railway?' would never have been considered.

Off the rails, horse teams increased in number to haul the ever-growing size of load created by industry, although the four-legged beast was not without problems. Harnessing the power of 20 or 30 horses to pull in concert was difficult enough, but one thing which could not be anticipated was their natural discharge of waste. So much of a problem was it that the manager of one large north-eastern heavy engineering business said as he surveyed his strewn site, 'We've got that much horse dirt in the factory, I don't know whether it will be easier to move the dirt or to move the factory'.

Unfortunately for rose growers, 1896 saw the easing of legislation and combined with the development of the internal combustion engine, the truck as we know it was born. Heavy haulage was still the province of the steamer, the power of the traction engine being unsurpassable in this field. Numerous haulage contractors had the odd one or two big locomotives to pull the occasional heavy load, but the father of heavy hauling must have been a man called Box. Not for him the rapid trunk service into the metropolis, plenty could do that. Eight or ten tons was not worth wasting his time over, but if you wanted to move 30, 50 or 70 tons—then send for Norman E. Box, the heavy haulage specialist. From his base at Ardwick, Manchester, his big Fowlers clanked their way all over the country. Ships' boilers, electrical transformers, castings, anything with weight, anything which would move, then Norman E. Box would move it. If he could not do it, it just could not be done.

They never travelled very fast but the Box road trains must have been an impressive sight. Hitched up to the big locomotive hissing steam and belching smoke, was the load-carrying trailer. A very basic piece of equipment, solidly made, a low slung platform having four, six or even eight metal wheels. No rubber yet in these early days, just solid steel straight on to the roadway. Next in line was the tackle wagon, pulling in turn the coal-carrying trailer which hauled the living van. Yes, four trailers gaily trundled along in the path of their leader and although Lancashire may have been the base, it was Scotland, the North-East, the Midlands and the South where the Fowlers worked. The drivers, as can be expected, were hard men. Black with coal dust, scorched with fire and steam, they worked hard but they also played hard. On a good day with a heavy load, 15 miles was all that you could manage to do but, as coincidence would have it, the journey always seemed to end at a welcoming hostlery. Copious quantities of ale were consumed in another cloud of steam and often the drivers had to sleep the effects off in the steamer's coal bunker as they were too drunk to find the living van. Next morning, bright and early, they prepared to make a start. It was the driver and his hangover who saw to the fire, the mate to the breakfast. After removing the muffler plate, on top of the chimney, which had ensured that the fire did not burn itself out, the raking, stoking and building up meant that in half an hour the boiler was blowing off steam and itching to be at work. Having dined invariably on steak and eggs, progress was recommenced but if that regulator was opened too harshly, the front wheels of the loco would leap four or five feet off the ground as the Fowler gave its best. Names like *Atlas*, *Talisman*, *Titan* and *Rover* were proudly affixed to reflect the strength of the vehicle but there was to be one name with an entirely different connotation.

All haulage contractors, from time to time, came into contact with the police who were endeavouring to uphold the law of the land. But getting done for doing 9 mph when your speed limit was 5 mph, or 14 mph when your limit was 12 mph, just seemed too much. The tail light, being a storm lantern, did on occasion go out but why did the police have to issue a summons every time? Box finally rebelled and decided that, no matter what it cost, he would get the finest lawyer in the land and fight. Mr Joynson-Hicks was the best and lived up to his reputation by being able to create just enough doubt about each and every case to bring a 'not guilty' verdict. Justice at last. The law may not have been

too pleased but Box was and to show his appreciation the name *Jix* was affixed to one of the Fowlers— power of another kind.

Having substantial contracts for moving transformers in the fast developing electrical industry meant that the Box steamers were kept busy. The railways could haul them so far, but from the railhead to site was Box's domain. It was not unknown when a crew rang in from, say, Glasgow to receive details of their next job for them to be told to run down to Bournemouth. 450 miles empty was a hard slog for ten days at a maximum speed, when coasting down the likes of Beattock and Shap at a hairy 20 mph. It took four revolutions of that little wheel before the slack in the steering chain was taken up, so ensuring the directional stability of the outfit even at this leisurely pace took a lot of nerve and skill. Running loaded was entirely different. Every decline saw the mate leap out to attend to the wind-on trailer brake, the only assured manner of slowing the outfit down. By shouts and gesticulations the driver could tell the athletic mate running along-side the trailer to apply more or less brake. It was a change for him from toting sacks of coal to keep the bunker full and then every seven miles having to divine for water. Not for the steamers strategically placed water tanks on the side of the road, but more a situation where any pond, stream or river assumed far more importance than the modern day filling station.

Box was not alone in the heavy haulage field and in the early 1920s the competitors were given the opportunity of closing the gap in the standard of service which could be offered. True, when compared to the Fowlers, they were tiddlers but the new Scammell articulated machinery transporters were an exciting step forward in heavy haulage. An enclosed cab and a windscreen, positive steering and rubber tyres, albeit solids, were real luxuries. Norman Box bought four or five of these for the small 12-15-ton loads and they were also snapped up by people like Wynns, Marstons of Liverpool, Rudds and the mighty Pickford of London. This old established carter had taken a long time to give up its horses but on entering mechanisation it had gone into it with great enthusiasm. Being a large company it was susceptible to the whims of big business and in 1920 was acquired by the Hay's Wharf and Cartage Company as a wholly-owned subsidiary. The name and identity remained, as did an increasing awareness in the importance of heavy haulage, a big change from their previous long-standing 'smalls' business.

Marston Road Services was fighting hard to over-come the virtual Box monopoly in ultra-heavy haulage which had created a fair degree of financial hardship to any competitors. To harden this fight they gambled hard by putting to work in 1929 one of the most famous vehicles in the business. KD 9168 was the first articulated vehicle able to carry a genuine 100 tons, a big brainwave from the Percy Hugh and O.D. North combination of Scammell. The prime mover had a large riveted frame and solid tyres all round, but what was particularly interesting was that the rear axle had four pairs of these rubber tyres mounted in a line. The transmission from the Scammell four-cylinder, 7-litre petrol engine, which developed a massive 86 bhp, led via the remotely mounted eight-speed gearbox to a countershaft mounted midway along the chassis. Heavy-duty chains then took the drive from the end reduction boxes to the large rear wheels. Three fuel tanks were necessary because of the 1 mpg consumption rate at a flat out 5-6 mph, the mate being kept busy having to hand pump the petrol up to the centrally mounted scuttle tank. The semi-trailer was a hefty double girder construction braced to the gooseneck by a pair of hydraulic struts with screw-jack locks. This gave the crew the ability to lift the load as much as 15 ins above road obstructions or to extricate the tractor's driving wheels from the depths to which they sank in the highway. The latter was a problem which was to remain with this beast for the rest of its life. Perched at the extreme end of the trailer was a small hut, the home for the rear bogie steersman. It was his job to control the direction of the 16 solid tyres supporting the back end and, to aid communication, a telephone link was fitted giving direct contact with the driver. In this one outfit an advance was made in heavy haulage motor vehicle design the like of which has never been seen again.

Norman E. Box could withstand the publicity of this acquisition by MRS but what he could not stand, in this time of recession, was the pressure inflicted by the Hay's Wharf Cartage Company and it, too, sold out and became a subsidiary, but once again retaining its name and identity. To Pickfords this meant that instead of being competitors of 'big Box' they were now partners, so with an interchange of staff at all levels some of the secrets of heavy transportation were quickly shared. Box remained committed to the old-fashioned steamers for the heavy work although the trailers had become a great deal more sophisticated. The load carrier manufacturers in this era included Dyson of Liverpool and Eagles of Warwick. Even Fowler themselves produced a very strong double-cranked low-loading trailer on rubber solids for Box, but the strongest trailer of the day came from Cranes of Dereham in Norfolk. Although strictly speaking it was two separate bogies, the 64-tyred 32-wheeler was normally run as one massive trailer with a rated capacity for 110-ton loads. The axles were arranged to oscillate about a longitudinal axis so that the wheels followed any uneven road undulations. 19 in by 3 in wind-on wheel brakes were fitted and when running together a pair of telescopic drawbars ensured that the rear bogie followed in the track of the front one. Cranes had obviously done their homework with this trailer for, 40 years later, their similar solid bogies were still the recognised way of

An interesting configuration of trailer is seen about to leave Trafford Park in 1906 supporting this large iron casting destined to be fitted in the ship *Lusitania*.

carrying ultra-heavy long vessels demanding low carriage because of their high centre of gravity.

The Box company were obviously impressed with the performance of their little Scammells and of MRS's 100-ton artic so, when BLH 21 came up for sale on the second-hand market, they snapped it up. It had started life as nearly identical to KD 9168, but on completing its first journey to Cornwall, the semi-trailer was left behind as a base for the stone-crushing machine it was carrying. Joining a fleet of heavy locomotives hauling drawbar trailers it seemed natural to stay as a ballasted tractor and proved more than equal to the Fowlers. In this form very little weight was transmitted on to the front axle so it, too, copied the starting leap of the steamers thus, when one of the drivers nicknamed the vehicle *Leaping Lena*, it seemed so apt that it stuck for life.

Heavy haulage in this time was real pioneering. It was not unknown even for the experts to encounter a low bridge on their route which just would not let the load through. No scratching their heads for these lads, there was no alternative to unloading on to the roadway, towing it under the bridge on skids, then re-loading the vehicle on the other side. Tricks like this did not endear hauliers to the general motorists and the railways, too, were more than upset about the erosion of their traffic by road-going vehicles. Their pressures prompted several reports on transportation mainly chaired by people who felt that the motor vehicle had destroyed all the beauty and peace of life.

The ensuing legislation created the framework of haulage laws which was to last, in modified terms, right up to the modern day. Most remembered was the creation of the dreaded A, B and C operators'

licences, but an even more important landmark in the Pickford destiny was when the four main railway companies were allowed to purchase equal quarter shares of Hay's Wharf Cartage Company. This, of course, meant that amongst other things, these railway companies were now the owners of Pickfords and Norman E. Box.

Even with stronger financial backing, MRS refused to be overawed by big Box and in an almost classic move they ensured the disappearance of this famous company. Whilst explaining what MRS did, it should be explained why they did it. Box had established their business so well that just their name implied a heavy haulier of great repute. Quietly at work in the Liverpool area was one Edward Box, not directly a competitor, but he did own a traction engine and his name was recorded as a business title at Companies House so, when MRS bought that business out, they were quite entitled to use that name. Hay's Wharf were furious that MRS had virtually stolen the use of their heavy haulage trademark and took them to court over it. But, even with the best of lawyers, this was one case they lost and MRS now had legal backing for their name of Edward Box Ltd. As the names were too similar, Hay's had very little in the way of options open to them, so with great reluctance the Norman E title was dropped and the vehicles repainted in blue and white. Pickfords may have gained a fleet of heavy-weights, but heavy haulage had lost a company of great pedigree.

Even in 1920 the most efficient way to move tank rail loco-motives, especially in South Wales, was to use Wynns Heavy Haulage who operated both light and heavyweight versions of the Fowler steamers.

Right and below right Norman E. Box's *Atlas* ending a haul to Bolton in the mid-1920s and needing full use of its power winch to get the BTH transformer to its final unloading position.

Below Surely a very early version of the adjustable trailer seen about 1923 on the quayside at Newcastle about to unload this Clarke Chapman vessel bound for Northern Ireland.

Left and below left The new articulated machinery carriers produced by Scammell were a big advance in heavy haulage, offering the luxuries of an enclosed cab and positive steering. They were soon brought into service by people like Rudds of London and even Norman E. Box utilised them for the smaller loads.

Left There was little doubt about what this Box outfit was hauling from Bury to Bristol about 1928, the 60-ton cylinder being an ideal fit for the Fowler rubber-tyred trailer. *Atlas* and *Talisman* seem to be losing a bit of water as they prepare to trundle off down to the West Country at a steady 15 miles per day.

Right R.T. Wynn standing beside one of the Welsh fleet's first articulated Scammells.
Below right The company still kept their options open by operating this Foden steamer of similar configuration.

Right Showing the innovative thinking of Norman E. Box, this Mammoth Major was one of only three eight-wheelers built by AEC in this manner. Seen in the works of C.A. Parsons in 1936, the 15-ton transformer was well within the capacity of the low-slung vehicle.

Above One of the two big Scammell low-loaders operated by the general hauliers Curries is seen in the Heaton works of C.A. Parsons in 1938. The 54-ton stator was hauled to Newcastle quay prior to being shipped to the other Newcastle in New South Wales, Australia.

Left and below left December 15 1943 saw *Leaping Lena* about to leave BTH at Rugby with one of three 100-ton 242 KV transformers for export to the USSR. Even headed up by one of the ex-Box steamers, the winter cross-country journey to Manchester docks was recorded as having taken ten days to complete.

2. The Ts and Pacifics

As the Second World War approached, heavy haulage vehicles were very much in a period of stagnation. True the chain-driven Scammell articulated machinery carriers were not capable of 40-50-ton loads with their doddlers (little sprockets) on but above that the choice of vehicle was limited. Some of the steamers were now close to 40 years old and definitely overdue for replacement, but, apart from the two 100-ton artics, they were all that was left to pull the heavy loads. *Leaping Lena* was now hauling a Crane semi-trailer similar to that used on the Box outfit and both vehicles now sported a different engine. Owing to the foresight of Nottinghamshire bus operator Trevor Barton, the Patricroft diesel engine manufacturers of Gardners were now fitting their modified marine engines into trucks. The two big artics proved far better vehicles for the fitment but using them to haul 60- or 70-ton loads was mainly because there was not an internal combustion engined vehicle in existence which could pull them. Heavy hauliers became obliged to try the Scammell 'Coffee Pot' Pioneer which, although designed more for military, oilfield or colonial purposes, was more than strong enough to haul this sort of weight. Its role was that of an off-road machine so to the heavy haulage driver it gave the impression of a big, slow, numb motor. But in the darkness of hostilities one bright light was the arrival of a very good tractor, albeit from overseas.

Even the name Diamond T has a mystical sound about it and when you add a Hercules engine to its description, the picture of a thoroughbred is complete. The vehicle lived up to its image. It, too, was designed as a tank transporter but with 176 bhp and 12 speeds in the transmission line, it had lots more power and twice the gears of its British counterpart. Only rated at 85 tons gtw, Pickfords quickly appreciated that two Ts in pull-and-push combination were man enough to haul the heaviest loads of the day. Weights were building up with heavy electrical equipment out of places like BTH at Rugby, English Electric at Stafford, Metro Vickers in Manchester and C.A. Parsons in Newcastle being regular traffic. Moving stators, and transformers up to 100 tons in weight from inland towns was not without problems. Cranes' modern low-loading trailers were strong enough but the axle weights on the solid rubber tyres were anything between 30 and 40 tons per line. The 100-ton artics also ran with massive loadings, the consequence being that at times they literally sank through the road surface. The driver could feel this by a slowing down of the outfit and his first option was to try to accelerate out of the soft patch. But even with the new high-powered modern American trucks, putting your foot down with an all-up weight approaching 200 tons did not produce a great deal of effect. The remaining option with a sunken outfit was to jack it out and then plate the road with steel sheets. The crews were kept on their toes for, once progress was recommenced, they did not want to stop again so the recovery of the equipment was done at a very sharp rate.

The highways authorities were livid about the destruction of road surfaces and large bills regularly arrived in Pickfords' mail. They were not all necessarily paid as heavy hauliers became experts in the examination of road surfaces. If the material used was at all sub-standard then the cost of the damage was contested with never-ending arguments back and forth. Whose fault the holes were was a matter of conjecture but, in 1945, the consequences of this lack of strength were shown to be quite frightening. To the crew of the Diamond T pull-push outfit, taking an 80-ton roll housing from Sheffield to Falkirk was a straightforward haul. The heavy load route was followed north and sleepy Boroughbridge encountered as a matter of routine. Crossing the River Ure had been done on countless occasions but this time the trailer sank whilst half-way across. Wally Scott, the driver of the leading T, quickly realised that this was no time to reach for the jacks and plates and told everybody to bale out and run. Hardly had the men scampered to safety when the bridge collapsed throwing one of the Ts, the new Crane trailer and, of course, the roll housing into the river. To put it mildly there was hell on. Britain was endeavouring to get over the war and losing one of your main north-south highways does nothing to aid transportation or communications. On top of everything Pickfords had to recover the pieces which, in itself, was a major operation. The Army offered their help, which was gratefully accepted and they in turn moved the river, or strictly speaking altered its course so that the part of the bed where the debris lay remained fairly dry. It was then the strength of winches which dragged the pieces back along the river and up the bank prior to disposal. The tractor and trailer were complete write-offs whilst the roll housing was wiped clean and found to be undamaged which was, at least, one item less to pay for.

The end of the war saw the end of the steamer; not submitting to the modern diesel tractor but definitely succumbing to old age. They had served Pickfords well, one of their finest hauls being as late as 1942. A massive 120-ton casting was hauled from Sheffield to Distington Engineering at Workington straight over the top via Woodhead. Four of the locomotives were required and at 12-15 miles per day it seemed to take an eternity but the load was delivered. The choice of replacement was still limited and although Scammell had revamped the Pioneer calling it an 80-ton tractor, it was still slow. The T was by no means perfect either, a claustrophobic cab, headlights far too small and a tendency to snap halfshafts if the power was poured on too hard, but it could pull. Rudds of London favoured the big Scammell-Crane outfits as did Issac Barries of Glasgow. Fellow Glaswegians, Youngs, had a rare Diamond T artic on their fleet but the biggest thorn which was to stick in Pickfords' side was to come from South Wales.

Wynns had been hauling since 1863 and 80 years later had built up such a big fleet that they could virtually tackle anything. As early as 1890 they had been able to offer a heavy haulage trailer for hire with a capacity for massive 40-ton loads, but by 1943 double that weight was fairly regular. The company was trying hard to get into the fast-developing electrical industry which was producing some headaches amongst its customers. The big Crane trailers could carry the weight but the running height especially with transformers was far too high. Out of the necessity to drop the load as low as possible came the concept of carrying it slung on lugs resting between two girders. These in turn

were located at either end on bogies so the birth of the girder trailer was seen. For the bigger jobs the load itself was hung between the fore and aft bogies and the first end suspension move was created. An Edward Box outfit is recorded as being the first combination to utilise this latter method of transportation hauling a heavy Metropolitan Vickers transformer from Manchester to Portobello, Edinburgh, in 1948. Science, as opposed to sheer brawn, was giving the heavy haulier a lot more power to his elbow but no amount of strength could withstand the sledge hammer which was dropped on the industry in that year.

The merits of nationalisation are best discussed by politicians but the end of the 1940s and the beginning of the 1950s saw a total upheaval in the industry with vehicles being bought and sold, repainted and redistributed back round the country. The Act of Parliament declaring government ownership specifically excluded compulsory purchase of vehicles used for abnormal loads, house removals, tankers, timber and meat haulage so, in theory, the heavy side of haulage should have been left alone. In practice it was destroyed. Pickfords, for instance, were owned by the four main railway companies and as this was the first method of transportation to be bought up it meant that they, too, became an asset of the country. Other hauliers also found themselves bought out because of 'other' reasons and some found most of their fleet compulsorily purchased whilst the odd heavy tractor they owned was excluded. The end result was that nearly every old company in the heavy haulage field just disappeared into the British Road Services machine although thankfully, for historians at least, two big names survived the major surgery.

The newly created BRS was split up into eight territorial divisions spread countrywide but owing to the influx of vehicles which were not really catered for in general haulage, a ninth division with its head office at Enfield, North London, was set up. Bureaucracy may have had its rules, but government officials did realise that you cannot just wipe out 300 years of tradition, so the division catering for house removals, meat, tankers and heavy haulage was, as we all know, called Pickfords. Twenty-six depots for low-loader work alone reflects the size of this specialist group but, in fairness, only a few of these catered for the very heavy traffic. Birmingham had always been one of Pickfords strongest depots along with Manchester and Sheffield, but come the revolution, Newcastle and Glasgow also slipped into this ultra-heavy league.

The transition for the men was a difficult time. One day you have your own boss and pride in your own company, the next you are just a small cog in the massive firm of Pickfords, up until then your biggest arch rival. Ill feeling got to such a pitch with the men from Edward Box and E.W. Rudd that, in order to appease them, the names of these companies were left on their vehicles, although the colour was changed to the Pickfords' livery and the lion on the door was BRS. Even the original Pickfords staff did not want all this extra manpower, extra depots and extra assorted machinery to tarnish their image so all in all nationalisation was not a joyous time, except perhaps for the Welshman. Having lost all their normal vehicles to the government, Wynns threw all their energies into abnormal load carriage investing heavily in ex-American tank transporters to do all the hard work. Twenty Hercules-powered Ts were the mainstay, but the most interesting purchase was six tractors manufactured by the Pacific Car and Foundry Company. The mighty Pacifics proved an impressive sight on the highways of the land but before they got to work, Wynns engineers had virtually rebuilt them to their own design. Being powered originally by a 240 bhp Hall-Scott petrol engine, the M26 tractor only achieved 1 mpg, so in the first instance the Hercules was fitted as an alternative power pack. The transmission was interesting in that the 6 × 6 configuration consisted of a normal shaft-driven front axle whilst the rear axles were chain-driven. Strengthened sprockets and crown wheels were fitted, along with a specially designed wooden framed crew cab and, as and when the vehicles were completed, they took to the road. The finishing touch by John Wynn, in true Box tradition, was the affixing of names: *Dreadnought, Conquerer, Valiant, Challenger, Helpmate* and *Enterprise*.

Coinciding with their arrival, Cranes built two special girder trailers to carry 140 tons or there-abouts, one for Wynns and one for the Manchester depot of Pickfords. What was mainly different was that the tyres fitted were at last pneumatics, the 16 huge 16.00 × 20 24-ply rating Goodyears ensuring a smoother ride for the load and a cushioned effect for the road surface. In 1952 Wynns threw down a gauntlet to the ninth division when *Dreadnought* and a pushing T carried the heaviest piece of electrical equipment ever moved by road. Using the big Crane trailer, 150 tons of BTH transformer, the first of six similar loads, was hauled the 70 miles from Rugby to Staythorpe in Nottinghamshire at an average speed of 3-4 mph.

Pickfords appreciated they had a challenge on their hands and their inherited old Pioneers were rather overawed by the impressive Pacifics. Thankfully for them, Scammell came to the rescue with a brand new design which was soon brought into service. The Constructor was of 6 × 6 drive and like its new 4 × 4 partner, the Mountaineer, it would be difficult to describe it as beautiful. It was not built specifically to look good, it was built for heavy haulage and the 12.17-litre C6NFL Rolls-Royce engine pushing out 184 bhp could certainly do that. Coupled to the six-speed gearbox was a two-speed transfer box so the 12 ratios gave the driver quite a turn of speed as long as he could stand the racket inside the cab. The big Constructor's arrival saw the retirement of *Leaping Lena* and KD 9168, both thankfully preserved for posterity. Box's 100-tonner had gone to Pickfords' Glasgow depot on nationalisation and there had seemed no limit as to the weight these two old vehicles could carry, the only constraints being the strength of the road surface they were travelling on. *Lena* was once recorded as pulling 180 tons internally in a Sheffield steel works and this was with the six-cylinder Gardner engine as well. Although the tractors were withdrawn owing to old age, their two semi-trailers fitted with suitable dollies continued to be used as drawbar outfits well into the 1960s reflecting, indeed, how well these vehicles stood up to the rigours of time.

Pickfords and Wynns were the leading heavy hauliers at this time but with the coming of denationalisation the 1950s saw a big growth in the competition, especially in the lighter end of the field. The London area had Annis and Co and Hallet Silbermans with Hopes at Bedfont, whilst Hills of Botley serviced the south coast. The midlands had Wrekin Roadways, Red House Motor Services and Starr Roadways, whilst Lancashire had Becks of Stockport, Walter Denton and Millers of Preston. Pickfords' Glasgow depot had strong competition growing right on their doorstep in the form of Gavin Wilkies, Glasgow Hiring and McKelvies of Paisley whilst the North-East of England was to spawn three major heavy hauliers which certainly gave Pickford's Birtley and Stockton depots a very hard time. In lofty north-west Durham, Siddle C. Cook's fleet grew hand in hand with the increased demand for Consett Iron Company steel and the number of licences he could get from the local traffic commissioners. Similar constraints were placed on the brothers Sunter, who were endeavouring to serve the Teeside steel works from rural Northallerton whilst midway between was a haulier just interested in weight. Crook and Willington Carriers were based at Bishop Auckland so, in theory, they were well placed for Consett, Tyneside and Teeside, an ideal location for their small fleet of Diamond Ts, Scammells and Fodens.

Cooks and Sunters had been competitors in both the timber and long steel traffic for some time and their progress into heavy haulage coincided as well.

Both started off with Mountaineers, RUP 900 and KVN 604, then in 1955 both stepped up to the big Constructors, SPT 600 and NAJ 920. Siddle Cook paid out £7,300 for his big Scammell and it was probably the only UK 6 × 6 Constructor ever to operate as an artic. Cook abhorred the waste of having to carry dead ballast around on his tractors and used the artic configuration so that the weight of the load maintained traction for the driving wheels. Sunters' Constructor reached an exalted place by being road tested by *Commercial Motor* magazine prior to delivery in 1955. John F. Moon recorded that he got 2.63 mpg at 85 tons gtw from the Rolls-Royce engine and it should be noted that the specification on the vehicle showed only Clayton Dewandre air servo brakes on a vehicle which could do nearly 40 mph and was to pull over 200 tons.

Compared to the hard-up private enterprise operator, who had to make do with adapting strong tank-carrying trailers for his heavy loads, Pickfords were able to afford the capital to invest in the biggest and the best. Working to their specifications, Cranes of Dereham produced TM 413, six axles of girder trailer with a capacity of 200 tons. What a monster! It was only one trailer but it meant that Pickfords could carry anything that heavy giving the spread of weight required on a girder trailer. The solid-tyred bogies offered this type of capacity but were no good for concentrated lumps like transformers or roll housings. Wynns retaliated and immediately applied for a licence for a similar 200-tonner and, of course, Pickfords objected saying they could meet all the demand made to move loads of this weight. Fortunately for Wynns both AEI and BTH, two of the biggest electrical manufacturers, supported their application, as they did not want BRS to monopolise the traffic, and the licence was granted.

If anyone held a monopoly it was Scammell whose vehicles seemed to dominate the heavy haulage scene at the time. Their articulated eight-wheelers were the standard for 20-25-ton loads, then the Mountaineer pulling a drawbar trailer came in

at 45 tons. The Constructor was good for 100-plus and in 1956 Scammells bridged the gap between these two by introducing a Leyland-engined 6 × 4 tractor. The Junior Constructor was one vehicle which could be described as almost beautiful, although in modern day terms the 150 bhp from the 680 engine would be thought of as vastly under-powered. Pickfords did not think so and, like several other operators, got a very good work load out of their numerous Juniors.

Wynns may have been impressed but were not tempted to change horses and persevered with their American contingent for even if it meant double or triple heading, the red Pacifics could match the blue Constructors. Both the companies offered equal capacity 200-ton trailers now, but Wynns were able to take a leap on the ninth division with the arrival into the country of the first flat top. Late 1957 saw a 160-ton capacity, eight-axled, 64-pneumatic-tyred trailer go into service made by Willy Scheuerle Fahrzeugfabrik of Germany. Quite a mouthful, but quite a trailer. In appearance it had similarities to Pickfords' old solid tyred bogies joined together with the 10-ton table. Both were automatically steered but where the Scheuerle more than scored was with its hydraulic suspension. At the touch of a button the running height was raised/lowered from 2 ft 4 ins to 3 ft 6 ins so loading and unloading was now a matter of seconds as opposed to the previous hours needed for jacking.

The gangs of Pickfords and Wynns were renowned for moving objects far and beyond the capacity of the heaviest mobile cranes, which were limited then to 40 to 50 tons, by winching, jacking, skidding and also adopting techniques that could not be found in any text books. The arrival of this new-fangled trailer did not change the requirement for this art but it certainly made things easier for the opposition. If this was not bad enough there was yet another competitor waiting in the wings to show how he, too, could out-manoeuvre the experts in a way never quite attempted before.

Left Woodhead 1942, Pickfords big Crane trailer and four of the big steamers in their finest hour, en route from Sheffield to Workington with this 120-ton casting.

Right This all Fowler outfit is seen at Rugby on October 18 1942 proving that these ex-Box vehicles certainly worked for their keep.

Right and below right The Diamond T pull-push combination with a Crane solid tyred trailer was Pickfords standard heavy haulage outfit of the 1940s. This Birmingham-based outfit is seen in 1943 with an 81-ton stator en route to Leeds and again just leaving Teeside in 1948 with a hefty steel fabrication.

Above As early as 1943 Wynns were using this girder trailer having a capacity of 90 tons. It is seen in 1948 leaving BTH at Rugby headed up by a very special Foden rated as a 100-tonner.

Left Boroughbridge 1945. The devastation caused to the bridge, trailer and Diamond T is plain to see, whilst the No Road sign seems to say it all.

Below *Leaping Lena* and driver Lowther, in the white overalls, about to leave C.A. Parsons in 1948 with a 124-ton stator for delivery to Newcastle quayside prior to being shipped to Canada.

Left and below left Two of the numerous loads hauled out of BTH Rugby bound for the Clunie power station in northern Scotland late in 1948. These pictures show the differing types of outfit used by Pickfords around that time. The old chain-drive Scammell is obviously happy on pneumatics hauling a 23-ton half stator frame, whilst the Diamond T is slightly 'over spec'd' with this awkward rotor rim weighing in at 30 tons.

Left Well thought out rigging of a set of girders and solid tyred bogies were made to ease the carriage of this BTH transformer on November 15 1943. Weighing in at 71 tons, it would be no problem for the Diamond T-Scammell box tractor combination on the short cross-country journey to East Kirkby, Nottinghamshire.

The first recorded end suspension move was this Metropolitan Vickers transformer which was hauled from Manchester to Portobello, Edinburgh, in 1948. The outfit is Edward Box's but the BRS sign on the side indicates that they, too, had already been swallowed up into the government machine.

At 110 tonnes this locomotive, destined for India, was the largest single exhibit in the Festival of Britain held at Battersea. The haul from Surry commercial dock to site in 1951 was the first outing of a Wynns Pacific and the company was extremely pleased with the way in which Fairfields of Chepstow had produced these special supporting beams at very short notice.

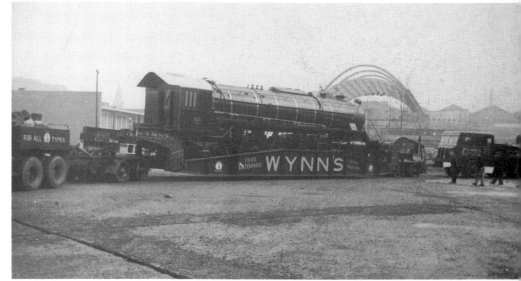

The Scammell tractor with four in line semi-trailer was virtually the standard 20-25-ton low-loader until well into the 1960s. This outfit, part of the Edward Box fleet prior to nationalisation, is about to leave Workington in 1952 and shows great faith in its winch rope.

Above left Jack Henderson checks security prior to leaving Stockton with this vessel bound for Birkenhead in 1953. There was no weight trouble for the 45-ton box tractor— the biggest problem was how to hang on to the attendant who wanted to bale out every time the outfit drove under some high voltage cables.

Above Seen in BRS (Pickfords) colours, this little box tractor belonged to the fleet of E.W. Rudd prior to nationalisation. The 37-ton Ashmore vessel had a long, bumpy ride ahead of it on these solid tyred bogies from the Stockton works to a BP refinery in Kent.

Left Birtley-based Norman Eaton drives down Northumberland Street in Newcastle on November 12 1953 with a 46¼-ton locomotive out of Robert Stephenson's Forth Banks works bound for Birkenhead. This immaculate Scammell, having a top speed of 16 mph, eventually finished its life working hard for Sunters of Northallerton.

Left Sunters first heavy haulage outfit, bought new after denationalisation, was this Mountaineer-Crane float combination. One of its first jobs was to carry this RB machine from Boreham Wood to Grangemouth, but driver Robinson had to take a circuitous route owing to height and weight limits. Every steep hill saw the little Meadows-engined Scammell run out of breath and a double head had to be begged from anyone passing. North of Thirsk the ex-BRS Foden in the background followed behind and hooked up when required. That arrangement worked for the rest of the way apart from at Coldstream, where a third vehicle was needed to mount a steep incline.

Above and right Master Raymond Cook sits on the flagship of his father's fleet on the day it was collected new from the Scammell factory in 1955. SPT 600 was probably the only Constructor ever to operate as an artic, a configuration prompted to cut down the necessity of having to carry 15-20 tons of dead ballast weights.

Above The DW registration might suggest that these Mighty Antars were part of the Robert Wynn fleet in camouflage. In fact they were on test by Wynns to demonstrate to their Australian owners that they were more than capable of coping with whatever the Snowy Mountain Range may demand from them.

Left Described as being the first application in the UK of a trailer manufactured by Willy Scheuerle Fahrzeugfabrik, this Wynns 32-wheeler had a capacity of 150-tons and heralded the start of flat-top hydraulically suspended load carriers. It is seen leaving Ipswich with the 77-ton base of an excavator en route to Heddon-on-the-Wall in Northumberland.

August 31 1955 sees this Manchester-based outfit on its two-day journey down the Tyne valley from Heaton to Swalwell with a 127-ton Parsons transformer destined for the Stella West power station. One of the 80-ton Scammell tractors broke down en route but the remaining two were more than enough to finish the short haul on their own.

A mixture of three gleaming Scammells wait on December 1 1956 whilst the Birtley crew jack down the Crane solid tyred trailer before squeezing under Walker Bridge on Tyneside. The 130-ton Parsons transformer was en route to Newcastle quay to be shipped to Liverpool.

May 20 1958 saw this mixed Birtley-based outfit leave the Heaton works of C.A. Parsons with a 78-ton turbine shaft destined for Canada. The smart Junior is being pushed by an old 80-tonner whilst the carrying is being done by a Crane trailer which was known by all who worked on it as 'the abortion'.

These pages Described by the media as being the largest load ever moved by road at that time, this 131 ft long, 16 ft diameter, 93 tons of stainless steel took three days to be hauled the 18 miles from Ashmores' Stockton factory to ICI Wilton in January 1957. Andy Higgins driving DUS 951, an ex-Issac Barrie Scammell, and the Crane solid tyred bogies from Pickfords Glasgow depot, managed most of the way unassisted. To surmount the 1 in 7 Leven Bank, two Birtley based 6 × 4s joined up; although the time taken to travel the 150-yard incline was 13 minutes. There was a tense moment at the steepest part of the climb as the 50 ft rear overhang nearly grounded. The outfit was stopped and planks placed in front of the rear bogie so that the load would be lifted when it moved off. The leading tractor had slight wheel spin as it restarted but the hardest part of the journey was eventually finished and the load delivered damage-free.

These pages The Wynns transformer trains of the 1950s were a regular sight in Rugby. *Dreadnought* and friends are en route to Staythorpe in Nottinghamshire with a BTH unit weighing in at a mere 140 tons, easy stuff for the six-axled Crane trailer. The 176 bhp Hercules engine did prove rather under-powered for these loads, thus requiring the use of three tractors although it was not surprising as the all up weight was close to 300 tons.

Above Ex-tank transporters were greatly utilised by most heavy hauliers not least Cooks of Consett. Siddle C. Cook also operated buses, an example of which is seen in the background. Close co-operation with Consett Iron Company meant free use of the occasional casting for ballasting purposes only.

Left KVN 604 is seen working hard in this scene from 1958. The 100 ft long pipe was destined for the number three Olefine Plant at ICI Wilton. The trailers used were ex-Army transporters.

Right Not a great deal of weight but still very awkward, this flame deflector is seen on the Roman Road at Greenhead en route from Ashmores at Stockton to the rocket testing site at Spadeadam, early 1958. A novel use is made of corrugated sheets on Sunters Foden which was fitted with a Gardner engine and eight-speed gearbox.

Above In 1959 this 30 ft high, 21 ft wide, 130-ton boiler was the largest yet to be made by Vickers-Armstrong at Barrow. It is seen in the capable hands of Wynns en route to the Buccleuth dock to be fitted in the *S.S. Oriana*.

Left The Rotinoff is seen leaving Hawthorns works at Darlington in mid-summer 1959 with the 150-ton capacity Crane trailer. The locomotive destined for export from Liverpool docks to India was similar to the load hauled by the Super Constructor when it was demonstrated by Scammells to Sunters at the end of the 1950s.

3. Bradwell and the Rotinoff

With the death of Joe Elliott, the vehicles of his company, Crook and Willington Carriers, came up for sale and as licences for heavyweights were like gold, they were quickly snapped up. Siddle Cook bought one of the Fodens, but Sunters picked up the other five, Ts, Fodens and a Scammell. This certainly strengthened the Northallerton fleet but the springboard into some real heavy business came along when the construction of Bradwell power station in distant Essex was being planned in 1956 and Tom Sunter was not the sort of man to turn down an opportunity like this. Head Wrightsons of Thornaby had been asked to tender for the making of 12 enormous heat exchangers for installation in the heart of the power station, the hitch in the contract was that if Heads agreed to build them, then Heads were responsible for the delivery of them. Even with modern day sophisticated equipment, a road haul of 250 miles of a vessel weighing 235 tons, 92 ft long and 22 ft in diameter 12 times over was out of the question, so transportation was to be quite a problem. Head Wrightsons were famous for their dock gates and the method of delivery used for these was simply to launch them into the River Tees then tow them by tug to wherever they were required. So models were made, tests carried out and when it was found these boilers could also be floated in water without causing any internal damage, the tender to build was accepted and work commenced. The only remaining problem was how to move them the 1½ miles on dry land once they had reached Essex and it was at this point that the brothers Sunter came into the picture.

BRS (Pickfords) Ltd obviously had both the equipment and the expertise to tackle such a job as this, but the manufacturer obviously appreciated being able to talk to the man at the top rather than speak to a manager, who would talk to an engineer, who would report to his superior, etc, etc. Sunters did not have the equipment at that time to do a job

like this nor had they tackled anything like it before, so it must speak mountains of the personality of Tom Sunter for him to be able to convince Heads that his team could do the hauls, but he did and the job came to Northallerton.

Sunters went to Cranes of Norfolk to supply the trailers for the job, two solid-tyred bogies each rated to carry 100 tons. At 10 ft 6 ins they were slightly wider than normal but it still meant that through each of the 16 little wheels per bogie there would be 8 tons transmitted to the road surface. The tractor unit was more of a problem as plans of the move showed that the boilers would have to be pulled out of the water on an incline of 1 in 10. Even with one tractor the all-up weight would be close to 300 tons so it obviously needed two or even three pulling to be on the safe side. Three Constructors would do, as would three Pacifics, even a combination of Sunters' tractors already in the fleet may well have sufficed, but on to the scene came a man who was trying to prove that his vehicles could do the job just as well as Scammell, Pacific or anyone else. Rotinoff might be a name remembered now, but in 1957 few people had even heard of him. His parents were Russian but he was born in this country and had grown up to be quite an engineer. Working from a small trading estate just off the A4 at Slough, he had designed and built on the lines of the Diamond T, a Rolls-Royce powered 6 × 4 ballasted tractor which he reckoned was the motor Sunters should have. The brothers must have agreed for RPY 767 soon came to shatter the tranquillity of North Yorkshire.

May 1958 saw the first heat exchanger leave Thornaby on its stopwatch-timed journey down the North Sea. The preparations on the River Blackwater included a special double wooden berth to position the boiler and a concrete strip to act as a slipway out of the water. When the tide went back, the two Crane bogies fitted with suitable cradles and connected by a central towing bar were reversed into position and anchored down. As the river rose and submerged the bogies, the waiting boiler was winched into the exact position alongside the berth. Held like this it gently sank, as the tide fell back again, right on to the two waiting bogies. When the tractors hooked up, the bogies were released from their anchorages and things were just about ready to go, although it did not go anywhere as the trailer brakes had seized. Even with lashings of protective grease, water had seeped into the lines making the system totally inoperative but, with no time to hang about, it was a matter of draining everything off and running without any brakes at all on the two bogies.

For the first boiler Sunters' own Atlantic was headed up by a further two from Mr Rotinoff's factory. Obviously a publicity stunt but if they did not do it this man's reputation was gone forever. Being prototypes all three tractors were different. Sunters' one had big single driving wheels, the other two had smaller twins. The rear axles had different ratios and the gearboxes were different. Undaunted, Mr Rotinoff had worked it all out and although a lot of thought and discussion had preceded the first pull it was still a worrying time. At the drop of Tom Sunter's handkerchief, the three Rolls-Royce engined Rotinoffs bellowed forth and, looking like something out of *Quatermass and the Pit*, the first boiler crept out of the river. Up the 1 in 10, the gradient eased to 1 in 46 then eventually levelled out. Here the two factory Rotinoffs were unhooked and John Robinson, with RPY 767, finished the haul alone at near to 300 tons gtw. It was a tight squeeze at times and a few trees were pulled down, also the odd stretch of road was marked as the Atlantic dug in to give itself traction.

Over the next 18 months the remaining 11 heat exchangers were delivered in a similar manner without the slightest of hitches. A varying combination of tri-heading tractors was used to move the boiler out of the river but normally they were the Rotinoff, the Constructor and an ex-Pickfords Pioneer, MUA 461. It reflects on the gearing of the old Scammell that, whilst the Atlantic and the big 6 × 6 both started off in 'crawler', it moved off in second. Much praise must be heaped on drivers such as Robinson, Fraser and Emms who, at the drop of a handkerchief, moved 370 tons dead weight on a 1 in 10 incline, using tractors with manual gearboxes and clutches, yet without a suspicion of transmission failure. In 1982 this sort of weight is fairly usual but 24 years earlier it was heavy stuff. John Robinson and the Rotinoff pulled all 12 boilers, except one. Running into Merseyside one weekend his instructions were to drop the loaded trailer and run down to Bradwell solo. He had only gone 14 miles when with an almighty bang, the

reduction gearbox seized up snapping the prop shaft and half the transmission with it. It was up to Jock Fraser in NAJ 920 to do the necessary with this boiler—300 tons with a Constructor is good going in anyone's books.

The transmission of the Rotinoff proved to be the weakest part of the vehicle. A six-speed main gearbox transmitted via a three-speed transfer box and the spread of 18 ratios gave the vehicle a capability of 48 mph. Sunters worked the vehicle hard as a lot was expected of it but it just could not take the strain. The tow bar proved to be John Robinson's best friend as he was barred back to the garage from all over the country. The teething troubles in the vehicle's first five years might have broken any other company, although Sunters hung on to it. In 1962 the vehicle was transformed with the fitting of a Self-Changing Gears eight-speed semi-automatic gearbox and went on for a further 14 years of very productive life. The Atlantic now graces the Transport Museum at Swindon, it being one of the few Rotinoffs left in existence. With the death of the founder no one fully took over his business, although Atkinsons eventually became the spares supplier and it may be worth comparing the lines of their ill-fated Omega tractors with that of the Atlantic. As it was the prototypes were left to stand up for themselves and Rotinoff just became a part of history.

Pickfords were probably the only heavy haulier which could have come up with a sufficient order to continue production of the Atlantic but, being something of an unknown quantity, BRS opted for the proven Scammell range the latest model being the Super Constructor. WYH 901 and 902 were two early examples being based at Birmingham and in concert with the Crane 200-ton trailer were a very impressive sight and fit to haul the heaviest of concentrated loads moved at that time. The Supers were a big improvement on their old 6 × 6 stable-mate, 901 and 902 having the 15-litre Leyland-Albion 900 engine. The supercharged Rolls-Royce was an option but the biggest step up was the removal of the clutch pedal and the fitting of the semi-automatic gearbox. Gavin Wilkies were obviously impressed and a gleaming example in blue, 473 AGG, soon came to grace the Glasgow fleet hauling their solid-tyred bogies throughout the country. With Wynns being inseparable from their American trucks, now using the Meadows engine, Scammells tried to encourage Sunters to purchase one of these new vehicles and asked if they could demonstrate their top of the range model, so a trailer and load were laid on. A lot of locomotives were being hauled both from Darlington and Teeside about this time, so one of these across to

Liverpool would suit both Scammell and Sunters. A brand new demonstrator came along with the best of Scammell's drivers and, although the weathered Rotinoff followed behind, the Watford men were out to prove their 6 × 6 was a better tool than the Atlantic. Any low-loader driver who had to circum-navigate Leeds on the heavy load route lived in fear of Rodley. The bank was not very long, but it was steep and right at the top you had to turn sharply. With artics the front wheels tended to come off the ground whilst with tractors it was impossible to get the necessary grip. The stone walls on the ring road were regularly robbed as drivers worried about ballast and traction but the Scammell pushed on undaunted. Sunters offered to hook the Rotinoff on behind but the Watford men, not knowing Rodley, felt this was an insult and tackled it alone. In fact it nearly made it, but close to the top traction was lost and in desperation the Rotinoff was asked to push. All that did was to dig a big hole in the ground as it fought for grip, for to stop on Rodley is a recipe for disaster. It took the aid of an old bonneted Leyland breakdown truck to head up before the bank was cleared, but this incident apart, the Super was a good truck and soon two of the Rolls-Royce version came into the Sunter fleet.

The Northallerton operator still failed to worry the big two who continued to try and out punch each other with bigger and better equipment. In May 1962 Pickfords introduced their 230-ton capacity ten-axled Crane girder trailer heralded as the most sophisticated yet, although the specification still showed that it had hydraulically-operated Girling brakes. Vital dimensions were: 89 ft 11 ins long, width variable between 9 ft 10 ins and 17 ft 4 ins depending on the load's requirements, plus an ability to drop its third and eighth axles if desired. In the first four weeks of its life it carried four trans-formers weighing in at 150, 155, 160 and 190 tons which indicates the work which was available to those who could do it.

In 1963 Wynns hit back with 'Britain's biggest trailer' again a Crane but this time on 12 axles with relatively small tyres and a capacity of 300 tonnes. Wynns' engineers felt they knew a thing or two about getting the best out of girder trailers and this one was made with the swan necks hinged on the bolster, an entirely new concept used for making easier adjustment to suit loads of varying width. The bogies were also detachable and great use was made of these when the big girders were not required.

Wynns' tractors had also taken on a new look, for with old age and rust striking hard on the Diamond T cabs they were replaced by a slightly bigger unit which was of different shape yet of characteristic appearance. New Cummins engines were also being fitted as the Meadows seemed prone to piston trouble, with the NH220 in the T and the NHRS 285 in the Pacific. Reinforcing the modernisation the Pacifics were fitted with the SCG RV30 eight-speed semi-automatic box so that there was now very little to choose between the Pacific and the Super Constructor. In the smaller tractor field there was now a new option aimed at ousting the likes of Foden and AEC for 30-40-ton loads. True, Wynns were selling Guys at this time but the Invincible was well liked by many others operating in this weight bracket. Both four- and six-wheeled versions were made, the Gardner 6LX 150 bhp engine being the standard power pack. Both Sunters and Cooks had several of these and both had a beefed-up version fitted with the 12.17 Rolls-Royce engine and ZF 12-speed gearbox, which was quite a powerhouse. About this time Cooks were getting good service from six left-hooker Super Beaver/Hippos and, although the drivers had to change gear with the wrong hand, they were a big improvement from the second-hand Scammells which were the back-bone of the Cooks' fleet. Pickfords oddly did not go for the Invincible range, preferring the Scammell Highwayman and some special snout-nosed little 4 × 2 Atkinsons for their lighter work.

However, heavy haulage is not just about tractors and trailers, engines and gearboxes, it is about men coping with loads and some of the tales which are told are frighteningly funny. Lol Johnson was driving Sunters' Constructor north on the A1 near Ferryhill with a high Kaldo vessel when he saw a large flash come from underneath the lorry, so he immediately stopped to investigate. What he did not know was that the power from a 60,000-volt overhead cable had arced down on to the load owing to the prevailing atmospheric conditions. An automatic cut-out stopped the flow of current but as Lol and the mates were examining the vehicle, the power automatically cut itself back in. It arced once more and, with a mighty bang, driver and mates were lifted off their feet and thrown into the hedgerow. When asked later what steps he took about an ensuing fire in one of the trailer tyres, Johnson allegedly said, 'Big ones. As fast and as far from the wagon as possible'.

Jimmy Golding and Jack Emms of Sunters must hold the record for taking the longest time to travel the 36 miles from Thornaby to Consett with the elapsed period being six weeks. However, it was owing to the atrocious weather conditions and not the men and machines which prompted all the delays. The snow drifts were as high as the leading Foden as the 98-ton load was mounting a steep incline near Tantobie when, without warning, the tow bar to the trailer suddenly snapped as a result of the cold and the big 100-tonner leapt away. Although Jimmy was pushing hard in his Diamond T, the Scheuerle trailer gradually slid backwards into a snowdrift accompanied by shouts of 'Chocks! Chocks!' from the Golding cab. Jimmy was known for his caution with big loads as he was well aware of the poor braking of the current outfits, but it took a certain amount of medicinal lubrication from a nearby hostelry before the crews could steel themselves to resume their haul to CIC.

For one particular big tractor to stand out wherever it went meant that it needed a personality and identity all of its own. *Leaping Lena* came into this bracket as did Box's 100-tonner but where there were numerous vehicles in the same fleet virtually identical then, to anyone other than the crews, they were all the same. Pickfords had countless Constructors and Wynns a posse of Pacifics, although 192, *Dreadnought*, stayed in the fleet for over 20 years and must be the most famous, but it is the one-offs which are remembered. Sunters' Rotinoff comes into this bracket as did the two big 6 × 4 tractors built by, and called, Annis. Arguably PPY 264 is also remembered by a lot for it, too, was very much a one-off. Fodens were well-known for their specials and this Sunter tractor could pull a genuine 100-ton load, provided you were not in a hurry. Its eight-cylinder Gardner engine drove through an eight-speed gearbox but where the big Fodens got their strength was through the use of hand-operated reduction hubs. These gave the ability to pull, but it also meant the performance of

the vehicle was that of a slow, ponderous, deliberate motor.

Out of all the Sunter drivers only Jack Emms had the personality which could accept and love this old tractor and he tells one story of the vehicle which I found impossible to believe but he swears is true. The local tyre man put eight new tyres on the rear bogie one day and, as normal, used soap on the beading to ease fitting. Straight out on to the job, Jack got as far as Six Hills near Bawtry, when he noticed that he had been alongside one particular tree for a long time, even bearing in mind the slowness of his vehicle. The engine was running, the gearbox was engaged, but even though the road was not icy, the vehicle was making no progress. The crew dismounted to find all the rear wheels revolving, but the tyres were stationary on the roadway. The liquid soap had allowed the wheels to slip on the beading and although the valves had snapped, they had self-sealed so the tyres were still inflated. The inner tubes had to be physically spiked and burst before the tyres could be refitted and, of course, from then on soap was never used in the fitting of new tyres on the lumbering Foden.

This old girl was strong but even all her power would not pull the loads that were to be moved 20 years later. The two decades following 1963 saw heavy haulage dramatically change with the 'big two' being ousted as the leaders in the field.

Seen in North Road, Darlington this Junior Constructor, with another Scammell pushing, is making steady progress for Liverpool with this 120 ft long Whesshoe vessel.

Above Consett Iron Company were not heavy hauliers in their own right but this shot, taken in the late '50s, shows how heavy haulage brings out the adaptability of normal road hauling equipment. This 130 ft long pipe had to be moved on site so the normal billet carrying trailers were utilised, the aft one in reverse form. The AEC Matadors were specially designed for CIC after consultation with Pickfords' engineers. They sported a Kirkstall drive axle and their usual bread run was to the mills at Jarrow, keeping them fully supplied with Consett steel.

Below NAJ 920 is seen entering Northallerton High Street with this 120 ft steel tower destined for a refinery in Lancashire in the late 1950s. Owing to bad bends in Thirsk town centre any long loads southbound from Teeside, like this 55-ton Ashmore vessel, were forced to leave the A19 and travel through Northallerton. The extra long drawbar was another Sunter special intended to inflict hernias on all who lifted it. Jock Fraser at the helm was most upset by having to drive this load through Manchester at midnight on New Year's Eve, a time when all Scotsmen get the call!

Above The first Bradwell boiler is seen in position having been winched to the exact point directly above the solid tyred bogies. The three Rotinoff tractors are seen waiting for the tide to recede in the top left of shot.

Left Once the tide went back, the tractors hooked up. Divers checked that the boiler had settled into the exact position then, with securing chains attached, it was ready to go. Mr Rotinoff is seen in the white mac waiting to prove that his three Rolls-Royce-powered prototypes could move 370 tons starting on a 1 in 10 incline using manual gearboxes and clutches.

There were always plenty of people on hand to give driver Robinson advice but, knowing him, he would follow his own judgement. The police escort had more trouble coping with the crowds than any vehicular traffic.

Varying combinations of tractors were used to get the remaining 11 boilers back on dry land. Here MUA 461 is seen backing up to tri-head the Constructor and Rotinoff. Tom Sunter is seen in collar and tie with Ron Allinson, one of the Head Wrightson boffins who conceived this method of transportation, being on his right.

November 1959, as the shadows lengthen the Rotinoff and the twelfth Bradwell boiler are shown in true perspective en route to the power station for the last time.

These pages WYH 901 and 902, two gleaming Super Constructors close to the end of a five-day haul in April 1960 from Davy United, Sheffield, to Consett Iron Company with this 170-ton roll housing. For the notorious Jaw Blades bank and other steep hills in northwest Durham PUC 472, an elderly Birtley-based 6 × 6, headed up the outfit making an all up weight close to 360 tons. TM 413 was an example of the strongest Crane girder trailer at that time, having a capacity of 200 tons and an unladen weight of 80 tons.

With rust and old age striking hard on the cabs of Wynns' Diamond Ts, the fleet took on a new look as they were replaced with a bigger unit, yet still of characteristic appearance. This outfit is seen leaving Rugby in February 1959 with the new Scheuerle trailer and a small Scammell pusher.

Dreadnought and the Scheuerle trailer used in two-bogie form easing over the old Green crossing near Newport Castle in 1960 as John Wynn offers instructions. The gantry girder being hauled is en route to the Uskmouth B power station.

Sunters' Rotinoff and 100-ton Foden go round South Parade roundabout in Northallerton bound for Erith in Kent, mid-September 1960. Even though it was running close to 20 ft wide and 180 tons gross, the traffic clerk badly underestimated the power of the Atlantic for, when it arrived at the Metropolitan boundary for the pre-arranged escort, it was seven and a half days early.

Right and below right February 19 1961 sees Sunters old Mountaineer on a round-the-houses move from Workington to Marchon Products, Whitehaven, with a journey time of six hours. The Scammell-Scheuerle outfit was obviously over specified for this 9-ton load, but the automatic steered trailer did provide the ample support needed to lift the 24 ft wide drum high enough to miss the lowly street furniture.

Right If Sunters were to haul this same mould from Thornaby to Consett today, it would be carried a lot closer to the ground even though the home-made semi seems well up to the job. This 11.3-engined Mammoth Major was well liked by driver Philip Braithwaite who said it would take 30 tons anywhere.

Left Jock Fraser punches Sunters' maturing Constructor through Bowes village on the A66 en route to Consett with the Kaldo ladle carriage which took up excessively long residence in Carlisle owing to a difference of opinion with the local highways authority.

Below Ted Stokes rides shotgun on VPT 85, one of the two Crook and Willington Diamond Ts bought by Sunters in about 1957. It is seen in July 1962 headed up by another T with an Ashmore Benson vessel en route to ICI Severnsides at Bristol.

Siddle C. Cooks quickly snapped up export cancellations which occasionally came on offer, like this Super Hippo due originally to go to Brazil. Changing gear with the wrong hand was no hardship to the drivers who thought the vehicles a big improvement on the large fleet of secondhand Scammells which Cooks favoured.

One of the biggest tractors in the Edward Beck fleet was this crew-cabbed Foden with prominent grill, a normal sign of the fitment of a Cummins engine. It is seen about to leave the Distington Engineering works in Workington with this hefty fabrication in about 1962.

Diamond Ts were extremely popular as medium weight heavy haulage machines but this Elliott outfit is a very rare artic version. This York haulier always managed to use semis to good effect. The Lima cab section is en route to Rochester in 1962.

Left Siddle C. Cook seen operating this ex-Crook and Willington Carriers Foden with a chain-pulled pole trailer en route to the new CIC plate mill at Hownsgill. The Gardner 6LW-engined tractor with reduction box also had hand-operated reduction hubs and was said to have enough torque to climb mountains provided the prop shaft did not snap.

Below left Twenty special loads of VC10 fuselage sections, hauled from Preston to Weybridge by Wynns, required a specially extended Scheuerle semi-trailer and this load was hauled by a very special Invincible.

Top right *Conqueror* and *Dreadnought* in concert are an impressive sight as they make easy work of this Ferranti transformer. The small-wheeled girder trailer was the first Crane 300-tonner bought by Wynns in 1963.

Centre right This freshly painted Birtley-based Constructor is seen having a storage tank loaded on to its 85-ton capacity Crane girder trailer on September 18 1963. The BSC vessel was transported down the River Tees by barge which meant that the road haul into Teesport was kept to a minimum.

Right One of the many Guy Invincibles operated by Wynns is seen en route from Darlington Forge to Uskside Engineering, at Newport, with an awkward 50-ton section which required carriage on a Wynns-built tilt frame.

See page 55.

4.Changing times

In 1964 Wynns and Sunters joined forces. Both companies suffered family bereavements and with ensuing problems over death duties coupled with the necessity to have strong financial backing for their operations, both decided to sell out to the massive Bulwark United Transport group. It was the biggest fear of all the Northallerton staff that the managing director in distant Chepstow would feel that Boroughbridge Road would prove an ideal base for a north-eastern Wynns' depot but, as it was, both companies were allowed to operate separately, yet with great co-operation over exchange of information, machines and manpower.

Along with this build up of strength in their competitors, Pickfords were having their own internal difficulties. On the face of it, 26 depots spread countrywide for low-loader work should have meant a virtual monopoly of all the work on offer. With the biggest and best equipment made, no one should have been able to hold a candle to them but, as each branch was run as a separate entity and each was expected to run at a profit, they were on occasion in direct competition with each other. This came about as not every depot had identical equipment and only the big five or six could deal with ultra-heavy traffic. Managers of all branches fiercely guarded their own customers, so even though another branch may have been in a better position to deal with a particular load, they were loath to part with the move, preferring to sub-contract and get the 10 per cent. Occasionally greater use of outfits could have been made to cut down emtpy running as, once again, branches were loath to give up traffic to their 'rivals' for back loads when the originating branches' vehicles could have carried it in due course. But with the 1950s and '60s being a virtual boom time in heavy haulage it did not make a lot of difference as there was so much work that everyone was kept busy.

The managers also had other things on their mind. Having battles with head office to get more and better equipment was bad enough but the structuring of promotion meant that quite a lot of very good junior staff could not get on because there were no vacancies. In sheer frustration they decided to take their talents elsewhere and lots of people like Sam Anderson and Henry Wood left the ninth division to join companies like Wynns and Sunters which were better off for the experience and expertise which they brought with them. Very little could be done to encourage budding geniuses to stay for, when in government employ, you are paid for your position and not perhaps for your true ability.

All heavy haulage staff had seen big changes in the industry in every sense of the words. The heaviest electrical unit moved in 1952 was 150 tons whilst 16 years later this had doubled to 307 tons. Dimensions, too, were growing with petro-chemical distillation vessels being stretched so much that 120-150 ft was not unusual. Delivering them had prompted development of stronger tractors and trailers with the latest bogies able to be steered independently, if sometimes by brute strength. What had not changed a great deal were the roads which these loads trundled along. Alleged damage to roads led to hauliers being given a rough time by some sections of the Press. For those of us who can remember the Great North Road in its original form, which passed through every settlement between London and Edinburgh, one can sympathise with the car drivers who were incensed at having to crawl along behind so many slow-moving heavyweights. The development in the motorway age of the Preston bypass and the M1 did not do a lot for heavy haulage for sometimes height and weight limitations meant that big loads were excluded. With industry building more sophisticated equipment it was becoming less easy to construct things on site so, from all directions, pressure was being put on the heavy haulier both to carry bigger loads yet also to keep them off the roads. The 12 heat exchangers taken to Bradwell was a classic example of how to achieve both these aims but it was fortunate that the manufacturer and recipient were both close to the North Sea.

The trump card which the Ministry of Transport produced was the law. In enacting the Special Types General Order they gave operators virtual carte blanche to carry at will loads within certain dimensions, provided the requisite paperwork was completed correctly. Once these limitations were exceeded, viz a vehicle of more than 150 tons gvw, 90 ft rigid length or 14 ft 1 in in width, then a special order granted by the Ministry was needed. It was far cheaper to haul by road a 160-ton transformer from, say, Edinburgh to Southampton, but the Ministry order was more likely to dictate that the only bits of road to be used were between the factory and the docks in Edinburgh, then from the docks to delivery point in Southampton. Joining these two hauls up was an expensive ship, but it did mean that one excessively large load could be built and delivered with the least amount of road congestion.

'Vigilant', a crusader of the 'clear the road' campaigners, wrote in the *Newcastle Evening Chronicle* and his column regularly reported the noise, damage and congestion which heavyweights were causing in the north-east. What incensed him most was to see a rail locomotive being carried on a road-going low-loader, which was hypocrisy indeed. On April 25 1956 he heralded a new era as a 135-ton stator was delivered from C.A. Parsons, Newcastle to Littlebrook power station, Dartford, with the mileage between the Tyne and the Thames being covered on a coastal steamer.

Being the largest heavy haulier, the pressure was put on Pickfords to work hand in glove with the way the Ministry was trying to satisfy both the large load manufacturers and motoring public. Under that influence loads from Sheffield to Scotland, the latter always the most difficult part of the UK for heavy haulage, took rather a strange diversion. With about a dozen ultra-heavy castings required at the Ravenscraig steel works, Pickfords laid-down route

was from Yorkshire to Liverpool and then by boat to the Clyde. Most of these were delivered without incident but one ship had the misfortune to collide with another vessel in thick fog as it was leaving the mouth of the Mersey and the castings sank to the sea bed never to be seen again. Even at Borough-bridge loads of steel were rarely lost without trace from the back of a low-loader, so on occasion ships do have their disadvantages. For those of you who are interested, the boat used on that particular occasion was the *MV Lurcher*.

County highways departments, always touchy about damage to their roads, started to complain over the use of solid tyres and apart from the heavy bogies, the 1960s saw the withdrawal of all the old Crane trailers. Even with pneumatics, bridges had to be regularly strengthened to withstand excessive weight so, if a haulier wanted this to be done, he had to ensure that the work was paid for. £5,000 went to one county council for just such a beefing-up for some heavy loads which were delivered incident-free into Scunthorpe. It was not until the job was finished that Pickfords found that only one side of the bridge had received attention and, as one might guess, all the loads crossed over on the weakened side.

Special order work for a haulier meant that he had to liaise closely with the Ministry, all the police forces and highways authorities whose areas he crossed, and also people like British Telecom, British Rail and, of course, the Electricity Board. Keeping all of these happy all of the time was sometimes not possible. Jock Fraser encountered such a situation as he drove Sunters' big Constructor into Carlisle one weekend in early 1963 en route from Workington to Consett with a 17 ft 3 ins wide ladle carriage, the all-up weight of which was close to 200 tons. The standard heavy load route through the city was too narrow so the Ministry-approved directions gave them a set diversion down Bocher-gate. 'You can't go down there' said the Local Authority, 'we've got road works.' 'This is a fine time to tell us' said Sunters, 'we'll just plate over the

holes and get past, it won't take long, we're used to doing this.' 'No you won't' said the LA, 'you'll wait till we are finished, we'll only be 3 or 4 weeks.' 'We can't wait three or four weeks' said Sunters, 'Let's be past.' 'You stay there,' said the LA. Sunters were furious for, as well as the load being required at CIC, the 150-ton girder trailer was booked for several jobs. 'Send me a load of timbers' said Jock Fraser and with no more to do the 80-ton lump was unloaded on to a city centre car park one night and the Sunter vehicles crept out of town. It was now the turn of the Local Authority to get upset and they insisted that the obstruction be moved but, until the route was finished and Sunters felt like recommencing the haul, the carriage went nowhere.

Pickfords had a similar confrontation in Manchester, not only with the council but also with the local police. They both agreed that the Regent Bridge just could not carry the 164-ton casting en route from Davey's at Sheffield to the docks for export to the USA. The Ministry pulled rank and said, 'That's our bridge, you go over it,' but the ensuing publicity meant that by the time the pull-push Diamond T combination reached Manchester, hundreds of people had gathered expecting something special to happen. The police had cleared everything and everybody off the bridge and all the attendants dismounted before the load started to creep over. Only the drivers were allowed to accompany the outfit and when it reached halfway the crowd held their breath. They were still holding their breath when it reached the other side for nothing had happened. At Ardrossan, however, something special did happen.

Getting large loads in and out of Scotland was always hard work. With height and weight limitations on the major routes, one of the standard heavy haulage diversions was the coastal route down through Ardrossan. The Scottish bridge authority had always hinted the Parkhouse bridge was weak but until about 1952, Pickfords never really knew what they meant by weak. 82 tons of bedplate and crankshaft were on the three-axled solid-tyred

drawbar low-loader en route from Greenock to George Clarke's of Sunderland. Saturday night was spent parked up in Ardrossan and the following morning saw a little chain-drive box tractor head up an ex-WD Pioneer as the outfit climbed out of the town and turned right on the A78. It was still a climb up to the railway bridge so there was no rapid approach and the Scammells crossed at a steady pace. But when the two rear axles of the load carrier got on to the bridge, the roadway collapsed and trailer and load went down the hole. Even the tractors were pulled eight feet backwards before momentum was stopped as the trailer hit the railway line. Another state of devastation. It was the railways which came to the rescue on this occasion as two 80-ton cranes were quickly dispatched down the line from Motherwell and Rutherglen. In no time the load and trailer were extricated and apart from twisted drawbars the outfit was damage free. The hole in the road and damage to the crew's nerves took slightly longer to repair.

Strengthening the Scammell range in 1964 came the Contractor. Not a direct replacement to the Constructor, which stayed in limited production until it changed into an eight-wheeled freighter, but a more refined model with more options to the potential customer. With a choice of AEC, Rolls-Royce and Cummins engines, the 6 × 4 chassis suitable for either artic or drawbar use could also be fitted with either manual or semi-automatic transmission. Two basic cab options saw a crew cab very similar to the Super Constructor whilst the smaller version had smooth, rounded, pleasing lines. With the plated weight of the strongest model increased to 240 tons gtw, Pickfords soon brought them into service as the fleet flagships. Double, triple or quadruple use of tractors in combination

One of two loads of roof trusses moved by Sunters from Newcastle-upon-Tyne to Peterlee about 1967 gave no weight or width problems to the Mammoth Major, although its 125 ft length made it particularly impressive.

either pulling or pushing had been a way of life for a long time, however, unless the tractors were matched exactly and the drivers worked in close sympathy with each other, the transmission of each vehicle could take an awful hammering, it being impossible to ensure that changing gear and braking were done by all the drivers at precisely the same time. The new Contractor would not be able to carry everything single-handed but Pickfords felt that two of these pulling and pushing could tackle nearly anything on reasonable terrain.

In 1968 they pushed the record of the heaviest load ever carried to just over the 300-ton mark when they hauled a C.A. Parsons electrical unit from Newcastle to Dungeness. No direct haul by road was possible here, either, as the North Shields to Folkestone route was covered by a vehicle which was not suited to drive down the A1. The trailer used on this job was one of the biggest of the day, a 12-axle Crane rated to carry over 300 tons with an unladen weight of 89 tons. With a full load, mathematics will show that the axle loadings were well over the 30 tons a line mark, which made the Central Electricity Generating Board start to worry. This load might have been the first 300-plus-tonner but loads of this weight were to become fairly regular and some old bridges just could not take axle loadings of this kind. Ships were used to their maximum but everything had to be hauled by road eventually and, as there was a limit to the number of wheels which could be put under a girder trailer, something had to be devised quickly which could reduce loading to a more reasonable level. The answer was a load of hot air. Known as ACE 1, the air cushion equipment worked on the same principle as a hovercraft for, with the fitting of a flexible skirt and overhead ducting to the trailer, the activating of a blower truck attached at the rear forced air down on to the ground in the area between front and rear bogies. The trailer did not float away but the creation of weight transfer meant that, when required, the axle loadings could be reduced to a more tolerable 20 tons per line.

Twenty years after nationalisation the politicians did it again. True haulage, and especially heavy haulage, was near to being a closed shop with those who were 'in' ganging up and objecting to any potential competitors. But at a stroke the 1968 Transport Act threw out the A, B and C licences giving everybody an O licence which allowed all to carry anything for anybody, without restriction. In theory this meant that Joe Bloggs, who used to carry his own coal on a little 7-tonner, could sell his Ford and buy a 100-ton Scammell then go for traffic which had been strictly the domain of the select few. Prior to 1968 there had only been a few own-account operators in heavy haulage. People like George Wimpey and some crane operators required their own big low-loaders, as did British Nuclear Fuels Ltd whose cargo of little white boxes, similar to electrical units, was very heavy indeed. Starting with ERF artics the Cumbria fleet strengthened their potential with two Rolls-Royce powered Contractor-Crane Fruehauf combinations that were known by the locals as 'Coffin Carriers' because of the load they carried. Their standard haul was between Windscale and Chapelcross in Dumfries at an all-up weight of 96 tons. Not a lot of weight was actually carried but the radioactive qualities made it essential that sufficient heavy shielding was utilised. There was little likelihood of BNFL wanting to back load with the odd transformer but the change in licensing did mean they were legally entitled to do so.

1968 was a black year in the Wynns calendar for another reason. Running out of Stafford with a 130-ton load due to go into store at Hixon, circumstances found their police-escorted outfit on an unmanned railway crossing at the same time as an unstoppable train. Running into this sort of weight something tragic was bound to occur and, of course, it did. Whose fault it was is not a point to be discussed here although the resulting ramifications were food for thought for anyone connected with the industry.

The late '60s also saw the arrival of big continental tractors from people like Scania, Volvo and DAF which even in standard form were fit to run at 40 or 50 tons with little bother. Beef them up slightly and an operator had a tractor which was economical enough to run in general haulage yet, when required, had the strength to pull some fairly heavy traffic. Investing in suitable trailers was not a problem either, for this period also saw rental companies offer low-loaders for hire on a daily, weekly or monthly basis. This change in circumstances did not take away the requirement for the specialist heavy haulier, but it did mean that a lot of his bread and butter stuff was literally taken out of his mouth. The big two were obliged to react to this influx of competition for, although they could offer the experience of years, sometimes the customer was only interested in the price.

Right 415 DAJ was the MkII version of KVN 604, Sunters' first Mountaineer, which was close to being written off after a bad accident on the A6 at Shap in 1961. The outfit is pictured on Victoria Bridge at Thornaby with part of a rotary dryer being constructed at ICI Billingham.

Above and page 50 October 29 1963 saw this 21 ft 6 ins high cooler and flame trap en route from Head Wrightsons to the National Gas Turbine establishment at Farnborough. After squeezing past a Stockton Corporation Titan (see page 50), the vessel was shipped on the *Leven Fisher* from Middlesbrough to Southampton docks. Two days were required to finish the 30-mile haul, although on this stretch the leading Rotinoff fractured an air pipe leaving the Super Constructor to carry on unassisted. This reflected the sense in having two top capacity tractors employed on an important haul like this, the 90-ton load being well within the capacity of either unit.

Left Used to very different types of police escort, Sunter drivers were still taken aback when these two single horse-power mounts guided this vessel through Stockton town centre on May 29 1965.

Below The police escort waits for 447 DPY and one of the Juniors as they bisect the town of Wells in Somerset. Sunters' 90-ton capacity Crane 32-wheeler is shown in narrow form which makes it ideal for the carriage of crawler bodies, provided the tracks are chained up.

The Constructor was the back-bone of the Pickfords fleet until well into the 1960s. At 70 tons this Ashmore vessel would prove little problem to the big 6x6 or the Crane solid tyred bogies.

Walsh's of Darwen seen making easy work of this crane section believed to be going from Dunkinfield to Consett in 1964. The well turned out Cummins-engined Atkinson configuration seems ideal for the job, although the two-trailer concept is rather questionable under modern legislation.

Barry's shop at Stockton got well used to looking at this 131 ft long stainless steel flash column which—on July 13 1965—was en route from Head Wrightsons to ICI, Wilton, because it took two hours to inch round the corner. Peter Sunter was quoted as saying, 'If the column had been just one foot longer it would never have got round, the operation was planned in great detail'. Not being one to exaggerate driver Robinson said 16 years later, 'It was a bit tight'.

Eight years after Bradwell, Sunter/Head Wrightson used the same concept of water-borne delivery for this 148 ft long column seen on site at Teesport. No big publicity for this but weighing in at 168 tons, it was at the time the heaviest load taken into the new Shell Oil terminal.

Total efficiency might be the heading of this photograph as the double headed Junior Constructors pause for breath and a fresh police escort on the trunk road near South Bank in July 1967. Sunters' solid tyred bogies are being used again and are shown to be ideal for the carriage of long heavy pressure vessels like this fractionating column en route to ICI Wilton.

Series One of the air cushion equipment seen 'blowing' on its first haul in April 1967 as Wynns deliver a 160-ton AEI transformer to Legacy, Mid-Wales.

Ten years after they were first introduced Siddle C. Cooks still felt the Junior Constructor was worthy of purchase, although by that time the power plus 680 engine was being fitted. The outfit is seen hauling a dockside crane cab section out of Clarke Chapmans, Gateshead, using two special 40-ton capacity Crane 16-wheeled bogies.

Late 1967 saw Sunters engaged in the delivery of this 120 ft long, 20 ft diameter, 95-ton fractionating column from Stockton to the Seal Sands chemical complex. Two Supers were needed to surmount Billingham Bank although, whilst the sedate pace did give the mate time to buy a pinta from the passing milkman, the drivers had to shout to be heard above the bellowing Rolls-Royce engines.

This well turned out Pickfords outfit is caught by photographer Alan Simpson negotiating Barry's corner at Stockton on April 26 1967. The big Constructor was more than capable of hauling this ladle en route to Consett Iron Company alone, but Pickfords were great utilisers of the little box tractor pusher in order to assist with negotiating tight turns.

Left Looking like some overgrown mushrooms, these 23 ft wide 16-ton dome sections were hauled by Strathclyde Transport Services from Motherwell Bridge Engineering to Hunterston power station in February 1969.

A tight squeeze for the Rotinoff-Crane bogie combination on December 12 1968 with one of two identical Head Wrightson vessels which had to cross Newport Bridge at Middlesbrough. The original planning of the route suggested there were at least 3 ins of clearance but, in practice, there was a flake or two of rust dislodged.

Known as 'the Polish vessels' because of their destination, this load was one of five identical tanks 22 ft in diameter, weighing in at 95 tons, hauled to Middlesbrough docks in May 1968. This spectacular Dennis Wompra photograph shows Peter Clemmett inching the Rotinoff down Linthorpe Road, although not all the shoppers were greatly concerned over its presence.

You had to have a good head for heights if you worked as a mate in heavy haulage. Sunters hard worked Super is passing the Five Lamps at Thornaby on December 20 1968 with this vessel bound for south Teeside.

Above Wynns' first involvement in Nigeria was the origin of this outfit which was known as the Rolls-Royce road-rail wagon and is seen leaving Head Wrightsons in 1967. This company made the massive girders whilst the Crane Fruehauf running gear could be interchanged with rail bogies to suit that method of transportation.

Below Running at close to 25 ft high this Whessoe vessel created a fair number of problems in its journey from Darlington to Consett in 1971. The entourage of wire lifters and arm wavers are being kept busy as the Contractor-Crane combination turns off the A68 at Castleside not far from its destination.

5. Widening horizons

The expression 'the bigger they come, the harder they fall' was certainly true for Pickfords who, for over two decades, must have been the leading heavy haulier in the land. But come the 1970s the accumulation of circumstances saw them prompted to close 13 of their depots. It was perhaps slightly ironical that BRS had recently bought out the Tayforth group who in turn had owned Siddle C. Cook since 1964. The Consett fleet was allowed to operate as a separate entity for some time but, being quite close to Pickfords of Birtley, it was one of the first casualties and took the Cook name into history.

Having a lot more freedom than a nationalised company, Wynns' answer to the suppression of the '70s was to go even further afield in search of work. Entry into the Common Market might have been a reason for trekking into Europe, but it was more distant places like Kenya, Nigeria and the Sudan which were to be the hauling grounds for the Welsh men and machinery. Cyprus was their first port of call in 1971 when a new refinery was being built at Larnaca. The island does not have the general need for a heavy haulier, so when some large boilers had to be moved from Famagusta docks, Wynns' Pacific *Helpmate* and a trailer were laid on to meet the requirements. Nigeria always had close connections with Wynns since the mid-1960s when they had been approached by the Niger Dam Authority to devise an outfit which was to be hauled by road, rail or water. It was Head Wrightsons of Thornaby who made the girder trailer and rail bogies which were interchangeable with the Crane Fruehauf road-going axles, progress being maintained on land by Contractors front and rear.

Wynns' main project in Nigeria was the organisation of transportation of more than 16,000 tonnes of equipment from Lagos docks to the Ashaka cement works in Bauchi state, a haul of over 1,000 miles. The heavy moves were done by the Wynns fleet who found the distance and temperature quite a change from their small, cool homeland.

Similar working conditions were found in 1978 on the other side of Africa and it is probably in the Sudan that the greatest amount of pioneering was done by Wynns. One contract lasting over a year saw them haul 1,000 tonnes of 'out of gauge' refinery equipment the 1,400 miles from Port Sudan to Rabak, south-east of Khartoum. The convoy of load carriers was accompanied by a mobile workshop, living quarters, 'chuck wagon', radio-controlled general utility vehicles and a motorised scraper, the latter to smooth out the 'road' when required. It made a change from plugging up and down the A38 with cafes and telephones on every other corner, for when they crossed the Sudan there was a light aircraft in reserve, just in case.

The red brigade may have been the most famous of British trail blazers but others, too, were wandering off wherever required, Pickfords' Glasgow depot obviously being able to brag of the most exotic of heavy hauls. On the face of it, moving nine units totalling 600 tons would be fairly routine but when the location is up the Irrawaddy from Rangoon and it is the rainy season then things take on a different aspect. Glasgow supplied the men and a 100-ton MAN, whilst the customer laid on the trailer, a 20-ton winch and the problems. The men arrived with the temperature in excess of 100 degrees so they immediately felt at home as it was just like the furnace of a Scottish steel works. Plans of the intended moves were changed immediately and problem number one was how to get some transformers off a barge which was running in far too high for the slope of the basin. Simple, of course, remove the trailer rear wheels and use it as a ramp on which to winch the load off the barge, up the slope and on to drier land. Further up river a railway track had been laid into the bank side so that the equipment being unloaded there could simply be winched straight from the barge on to the rail bogies. However, with the river subsiding, the railway line was too short, the mud was too deep, the rain was too heavy and, to cap it all, the customer's winch broke. Ye of little faith can still rely on Pickfords, for the enterprising crew found an ancient Scammell boom wagon just lying about waiting for such an emergency. With the fitting of a new wire winch rope the problems were surmounted and the loads delivered, of course. The men and MAN returned to Scotland although memories of this haul would never be forgotten.

It is Pickfords Rugby branch who must brag of having the fastest moving heavy haulage trailers in the land. The Crane Fruehauf drawbar trailers look fairly innocuous and on the memorable move they were carrying just over 30 tonnes each of electrical cylinder bodies. Bound for Taiwan, their customer decided he wanted them as soon as possible,, so flying was the only answer. A USAF military transport C5A Galaxy, nicknamed *Fat Albert*, an example of the largest cargo aircraft in the world, swallowed up the trailers and loads after being expertly pushed up the 1 in 4 loading ramp by a ballasted Atkinson. Leaving Mildenhall on the Sunday, it flew via Alaska and Japan arriving in Taiwan three days later. It is amazing what tricks heavy hauliers get up to.

For those with their feet on the ground, the early '70s meant North Sea oil and Nicholas. The modular trailer was here to stay and although the German company Scheuerle were the early leaders, it was the French Nicholas concern who were to come up on the rails. Cranes of Dereham had produced some small-wheeled bogies but obviously with a limited national market it must have been difficult to justify investing heavily in the research of this new concept. Kings produced some six row bogies for Pickfords but unfortunately these were not without their problems, thus it was open to the Frenchman who seemed to get everything right. Two basic versions, light or heavyweight, were offered and, as well as being able to add on axles ad infinitum lengthways, some trailers were made to be split in half widthways. With suspension and steering of all wheels down to highly sophisticated hydraulics, these new load carriers were the answer to nearly every heavy hauliers question. They were expensive but it did mean that if a company bought, say, 20 rows they could have any permutation of these axles lengthways or sideways which made them adaptable for nearly every conceivable job. Nicholas also produced trailer beds and adjustable goosenecks so general heavy haulage artics could also be purpose-built in true Meccano fashion.

Modular trailers were soon in demand as the heavy engineering companies began building hard in the race for oil. Assembling a rig deep in the North Sea needed entirely different building techniques to suit the environment. Once the framework had been sunk in situ, it was ready to receive its fittings which had been preassembled on shore like giant Lego building bricks. It was a straightforward matter for the deep sea crane to lift these off the barge and place them in position but to get these modules on to the barge the new trailers were necessary. It was not practical for every construction site to have suitable craneage to lift anything up to 2,000 tonnes, so the demand was made for the specialised heavy transporter to enter this field moving items around the site or on to barges and ships which, in turn, ferried them out to the rigs. Both Pickfords and Sunter Brothers were ideally placed to service the northern yards but, as the heaviest loads they had moved in the past were around the 300-ton mark, the prospect of moving items nearly ten times that weight was rather frightening and initially they shied away from this work as they felt they were out of their depth.

Being such a specialised entity, 'load-outs' prompted the forming of an entirely new company in the heavy hauling scene, the aptly named Magnaload. Owned jointly between Peckstons of Middlesbrough, who were in the shipping business, and Mammoet Transport BV of Amsterdam, probably the biggest heavy haulier in the world, its three-vehicle fleet of two 6 × 4 Volvos and a second-hand Contractor would hardly overawe the big two, but virtually the first haul it made put it into the record books. Four modules weighing in total nearly 7,000 tonnes were loaded-out on to barges in the River Tyne at the William Press Howden yard at Wallsend and the tractors did not even break into a sweat.

Archimedes would be the first to agree that you cannot just push a 2,000-ton lump on to a 300 ft long barge without something happening, so, to compensate for his principle, numerous pumps moved around the pre-loaded water ballast into different compartments inside the barge and eventually back into the river. As well as the transfer of weight, due compensation also had to be made for the rise in tide, it being unthinkable to try and load-out with the tide falling. Magnaload's method of moving this sort of weight slowly on to the barge or around the site relied on the strength of winches either mounted on the back of the tractors or welded to the floor of the barge with at least two pulling whilst another two were releasing, but always being ready to brake or retrieve if the circumstances dictated. Magnaload were able to offer the know-how for managing moves like this and being able to call on the equipment owned by the Mammoet organisation, which was anything down to tugs and barges, a lot of work was to come their way.

Rigging International, an American-based company, were also active in this field but their approach was slightly different in that they preferred to use crawlers. Looking something like the base of a large crane, these self-contained units were simply driven under the load and carried it about to wherever it was wanted, thus cutting out the need for trailers, tractors and winches. One of their drawbacks, however, was that they did not have hydraulic suspension, so loading and unloading were laborious separate jacking procedures. It was to be this handicap which persuaded Rigging to sub-contract some of their moves, so allowing Sunters a taste of heavy haulage, load-out style. Transporting this sort of weight was not difficult to do, if you knew what you were doing. The Dutch and Americans knew how to do it, as did Messrs Duffield, Wilson and Pearson.

These three ex-Rigging employees pooled their money and set up business offering for sale their expertise in the load-out field under the banner of ITM. They did not have any equipment at this time so, in the first instance, they went to Pickfords to hire the men and modular running gear to do the actual physical work when the loads were to be moved. But it was the structure of the blue brigade which was to create difficulties with ITM. Having so many depots, their new Nicholas axles were spread country-wide, so getting 30 rows together all at the same time for a load-out meant bringing eight rows from Birtley, ten from Glasgow, six from somewhere else, and so on. Once they had been assembled on site they had to be rigged up and tested which in itself was a lengthy process so, to a go-ahead young company like ITM, Pickfords seemed just a little bit slow. Unlike Pickfords, all Sunters' new axles were based at Northallerton so producing 20 or 30 rows was little problem and, of course, if desired Wynns could help out if they ran short. Peter Sunter had been champing at the bit trying to get back into the load-out field when Sunters and Rigging had both agreed to part company so, when the chance came up in 1977 to inaugurate the Sunter-ITM combine, he leapt at it, just in time to bid for the Shetlands.

The giant oil terminal being built at Sullom Voe presented a challenge to all concerned, BP the terminal manager acting on behalf of 32 participant oil companies and Constructor John Brown, the managing contractor. The extreme weather conditions, combined with the sheer isolation of the huge site, virtually dictated to CJB that wherever possible the major units for installation should be prefabricated. In fact 40 per cent of the process

facilities were pre-assembled in module form weighing anything up to 500 tonnes each and it was later calculated that two million man hours had been saved on site by utilising this form of building concept. Sunter-ITM's first contract was for the delivery of 37 pip255racks which were designed as linkable modules each approximately 72 ft long, 50 ft wide, 65 ft high and tipping the scales at 300 tonnes. The delivery timetable was highly concentrated and involved up to six individual racks being loaded-out on to one barge at the same time. From Leith, Tyneside and Teeside the flat-topped carrier set out northwards but such was the delicacy of the racks' specification, they could not tolerate any longitudinal deflection (they must not be allowed to warp) greater than 18 mm which, to you and me, means less than an inch. To compensate for such problems this form of heavy transportation can be very lucrative indeed. The distances involved are very short, but the weights carried are astronomical.

Following their success in the Shetlands Sunter-ITM went from strength to strength in the load-out field. It was mainly North Sea oil work, but one slightly different job was the moving of the Thames barrier gates from the Cleveland Bridge fabrication yard on Teeside. Not particularly high, the four main gates were nearly 200 ft long and weighed in at a hefty 1,500 tonnes each but the hydraulic suspension of the Nicholas trailers proved ideal to lift, carry and unload them on to the moored barge with little difficulty.

Since 1964 Sunters had always seemed to be the junior partner when compared to Wynns in BUT heavy haulage, but entering the '80s when the recession in road haulage began to bite, it was the Northallerton company which was to be the group's shining light. 1980 saw the SB-ITM combine take their expertise to the Persian Gulf. Sufficient contracts were won to justify a respray and a long journey for Contractor HVN 397N and a 6 × 4 Volvo tractor plus 20 rows of Nicholas running gear. They looked more like vehicles of a UN peace-keeping force. Gone was the distinctive grey and maroon colouring; white was now the predominant colour. A round badge on the door of the vehicles proclaimed they were part of the Hercules International Transport Co Ltd, this being a joint venture set up by Sunters, ITM and an agent from Dubai. One of the jobs the combine did warranted high precision know-how and was just a bit beyond the usual Arab or even British haulier. This entailed the moving of six massive balls or, to give them their correct title, pressure surge spheres, from the CMP fabrication yard at Ajman via barge to Zirku Island and then a 2-mile haul to their destination. Each was 200 tonnes in weight and 53 ft in diameter so that even the mighty Contractor was dwarfed by its charge. The trailers were fitted with a cocquetier to accept the radius of curvature of the sphere, it being specially arranged so that pressure was equally distributed and damage to the sphere's fittings avoided. Loading and unloading was done solely by using the stroke integral in the Nicholas suspension and the final deposit was done to such fine tolerance that it discounted completely the need for any heavy lift craneage. Yet another notch on the SB-ITM handle.

As Sunters and ITM were going from strength to strength, the fate of Magnaload took an interesting turn. Their destiny should have been sealed when Peckstons, one of their joint owners, went into liquidation but one Tom Llewellyn decided he might be able to do something about it. Since he had taken over as managing director of Econofreight Transport in the early '70s he had changed both the image and traffic load of this Transport Development Group company. The general haulage vehicles were still there but the tippers had gone and in their place were long load and heavy haulage outfits. Also operating out of Teeside he was well aware of the

prowess of Magnaload. It was certainly a very small fleet, but it was the quality of their equipment and the know-how of the staff which held great appeal, so out of the ashes of Magnaload in 1980 came the joint venture of Mammoet-Econofreight. Initially a 50-50 set up, but as the Middlesbrough staff found their feet, two years later the name had not changed, although Econofreight was the predominant partner. Their operation was similar to that of Sunter-ITM in that both companies helped each other either with equipment or expertise but Mammoet could also offer hauling facilities for traffic destined for Europe and their sea fleet was best described as large.

Teeside was thus the base of two of the heaviest movers in Europe. From humble beginnings ITM had developed into a company which Britain could be proud of, they may have respected Mammoet but were not overawed by them. The change in circumstances have meant that the big two of the '60s have now been replaced by the two massive movers of the '80s. Pickfords and Wynns may have been overshadowed but they were not written off.

Below left Hauling 511 tons in three lots from Birkenhead in 1971 was a big job even for Wynns for, at the time, they were the largest loads ever moved by road. Up to 28 ft in diameter, 111 ft long and 212 tons in weight, they required most of the road and a lot of police attention in the 17-mile haul to the Shell refinery at Stanlow.

Below right Seen approaching Newport Bridge, these 28 ft wide 110-ton half sections of a converter were quite a handful. Destined for the BSC Anchor project at Scunthorpe, the motoring public were bound to be pleased that between Middlesbrough and Lincolnshire they were carried on board the double hulled *Gloria Siderum* thus cutting traffic chaos to a minimum.

Above left South Wales is a testing place for heavy haulage. This 220 tonnes stator from AEI Manchester needed four of Wynns' biggest tractors to get it up the 1 in 6 Buttrells Hill when being hauled from Barry dock to Aberthaw power station.

Above right British Nuclear Fuels operated two of these Rolls-Royce-powered Contractor-Crane Fruehauf combinations in the '70s out of Windscale and Chapelcross. Because of the hazardous white boxes they carried, West Cumbrians nicknamed them 'Coffin Carriers'.

Below During the mid-1960s, *Dreadnought* received a massive face lift and had more than its share of Scammell bits under the Pacific skin. It is seen hauling seven rows of Nicholas bogies supporting an old loco destined for preservation.

One of Wynns 300-ton capacity Crane trailers seen entering the Davy Roll Company at Sheffield in August 1974 with this 195-ton casting from Germany. The three tractors, headed up by the modified *Dreadnought*, had to work hard crossing the Pennines from Manchester docks with an all up weight close to 400 tons.

One of the record-breakers carried by Sunters was this 228-ton steel column having an impressive length of 174 ft. November 10 1975 saw HVN 397N and 14 rows of Nicholas on its fairly short road haul from Tees dock to ICI Wilton.

Below A good example of the modern day Pickfords heavy haulage outfit — Contractors pulling and pushing TM 1120, 12 axles of 300-ton capacity Crane Fruehauf trailer. Seen in 1973, not exceding the speed limit, they are taking one of 12 167-ton low pressure steam turbine rotors from GEC Manchester to GEC Rugby for overspeed testing prior to export.

An early experience for Sunters in the load-out field was the site haul of eight modules each approximately 75 ft × 35 ft × 26 ft and 380 tons in weight. The odd layout of the Nicholas running gear was needed to turn the vessels prior to them reaching the water edge.

An early Detroit-powered Contractor artic of Heanor Haulage shows how the modular semi-trailer can carry excessively heavy loads, provided the weight can be placed over the axles.

Made of Wolsingham Steel, shaped by Sunderland Forge and hauled by Olivers Fodens, this 40-ton ship's rudder is seen leaving the Wearside works en route to Brazil.

Above left and right Sunters Titan I and Nicholas tri-axle semi-trailer is seen in 1978 with two very impressive loads. VVN 910S was made by Titan Gmbh of Appenweier, West Germany and the outfit cost Sunters in excess of £100,000 when bought new in 1977.

Centre left and left XUP 999F was the last big Scammell to be bought by Siddle C. Cooks of Consett before they disappeared from the heavy haulage scene completely. It ended up with Northern Ireland Carriers, a Pickfords offshoot, and is seen in December 1977 helping Magnaload into the record books. Built by GEC Larne, this 120 ft long 401 tonnes moisture separator-reheater vessel contained 35 miles of tubing and, when bound for San Onofre nuclear power station in California, it was the heaviest load moved on roads in the United Kingdom.

Above With the choice of either paying £15,000 for the removal of street furniture in Newcastle or £1,100 for the exclusive use of the Tyne Tunnel, Econofreight obviously chose the latter method in order to get this 50-ton Richardson of Darlington fabrication north of the River Tyne. This photograph, taken at 2 o'clock in the morning, shows what a tight fit the load was. Econofreight knew they could get it through, however, because with good foresight and planning they had taken a wooden replica modelled to the exact dimensions of the real load through without any trouble, although driver Steve Ford only had 3 ins clearance on either side. Doing the haul is the much modified DAF 2800 which is fitted with an Allison automatic gearbox, hauling Nicholas axles.

Below Middlesbrough transporter bridge, itself a great invention, looks down on this Econofreight outfit seen about to leave for North Wales. Getting these empty boxes to Air Products at Wrexham was impossible until this concept of end suspension was devised; although there was no weight problem for the ballasted 110-ton capacity DAF.

Above At 370 tonnes, this vacuum distillation column was the heaviest and most impressive of the loads hauled into the Lindsey oil refinery by Pickfords in August 1978. Its 40 ft height necessitated the removal of 42 lamposts and the raising of an NCB conveyor belt 21 ft to afford passage.

Left These spectacular Golf Oil photographs show a very awkward 220-ton vacuum distillation column entering the Milford Haven refinery in 1977. Eight double rows of Scheuerle running gear plus two thirds of the Magnaload fleet were needed for the job due to the all up weight being in excess of 300 tons.

Below Roy Brandley keeps a watchful eye on this awkward vessel as he steers the Nicholas on to the wrong side of the dual carriageway at Stockton, late in 1978. Econofreight like the four-deck-four trailer and use it a lot when rigidity between bogies is required.

Above Pickfords are probably the most famous name in house removals but Econofreight show how they can do it in a slightly different manner. The automatic steering on the Nicholas semi-trailer is shown to good effect as the outfit rounds Stranton roundabout in Hartlepool late in 1978.

Above left and left 712E was an example of the first batch of 240 Contractors to be operated by Pickfords after their introduction. The Scammell is easing out of Foster Wheelers at Hartlepool early in 1979 with a waste heat boiler destined for Immingham, all up weight being close to 250 tons. Left-hooker 925T, a MkII version, was only one week old when it headed up to ease passage over Newburn Bridge.

Above The MACK Interstater found favour with quite a few operators in the middle range of the business, Baldwins of Stockton operating two of these 100-tonners. They mainly used them in the carriage of their own crane equipment, but the openess of the O licence meant they could haul for others when site operations were quiet.

Right TSL get good service from their fleet of Volvos, this F89 making easy work of the NCK crawler crane en route from Middlesbrough to Essex. The King semi-trailer did need a helper tag axle to spread the weight of 89 tons which the combination was grossing.

Right With all the big Sunter tractors employed elsewhere, Wynns were asked to help out with a short haul to Hartlepool docks of this 180-ton Foster Wheeler package boiler in early 1979. Bound for the Texaco refinery in Pembroke, the load required very careful carriage which meant an easy time for *Invincible* and a cold crawl for the police escort.

Left March 1979 saw Sunters aptly named *Fearnought* engaged in the haul of one of three silos to ICI Wilton. Although the vessels had been manufactured at Dock Point, Middlesbrough, they had to be transported down the Tees by barge to Teesport so that the eventual road haul was kept to a minimum. The Cummins-engined tractor was hauling 16 rows of Nicholas bogies with 256 tyres to support the 98 ft long, 50 ft diameter vessel, all up weight being 343 tons.

Below Wynns 13-year-old Contractor heads up Whessoe's younger Scammell on one of the testing gradients in the heart of the Elidir mountain hauling steel lining pipes, an integral part of CEGB's Dinorwic power station, North Wales, April 1979.

6. Horses for courses

Into the '70s the Contractors became established as the leader in the UK heavy haulage locomotive field. Even Wynns returned to conformity in 1966 for, when their hard-worked Pacifics and Diamond Ts required replacing, it was the new Scammell range which took their place. *Dreadnought* received a massive face-lift and a new registration about this time but, although it continued to work hard for its keep, its days were numbered. The manufacturer's plate affixed to the strongest Scammell said that it was designed to haul a gross combination weight of 240 tons, but what it could actually pull safely was anyone's guess. The makers were not interested in changing the figures on the plate, although they liaised closely with operators who wished to operate at weights in excess of this amount. This seems a strange statement to make but two vessels moved by Sunters in February and April 1977 were a point in question.

Manufactured by Foster Wheelers of Seaton Carew, their eventual destination was only a few miles south on the big Seal Sands chemical complex but, owing to their massive 376 tonnes weight, they had to be road-hauled north to Hartlepool docks then ro-ro'd back across the Tees bay. If the tonnage was not bad enough, each vessel measured 92 ft long and 31 ft in diameter, dimensions which meant drastic modifications to the street furniture on the 4-mile road haul. One of these alterations was the swivelling round of all the street lights so that instead of shining on to the roadway, they faced outwards and illuminated the grass verges. With only two months separating the hauls of the two, the streetlights were just left in this position after the first job was done. Motorists did not suffer a great deal from any lack of light, but they did make numerous 'phone calls to the local police to report that 'vandals' had turned round all the lamposts on the Seaton Carew road. To get the best stability and weight distribution, Sunters' engineers decided to utilise two Nicholas bogies but, following load-out techniques, the 2 × 7 row configuration ran at a width of 19 ft and had 12 tyres per row. They were, in fact, an example of the Nicholas trailer and a half running side by side whilst a 1 ft spacer held things in position. Adding everything together the all-up weight including tractors was 634 tons, this was, of course, a calculated weight for even Cleveland Police would have been hard pushed to find a suitable weighbridge to check it. What pulled them? Contractor LAJ 798P with Bill Jamieson at the wheel, all on its own. True, Peter Clemmett in NAJ 103P did double-head over Newburn Bridge, but this was just as much to control the descent as to aid in surmounting the initial incline. Watching the Contractor travel along the Tees Road, the serene ease of its passage conveyed the impression that it was pulling something like 60 tonnes instead of over 600. In fact, there was far more smoke coming out of the cab window from burning tobacco than was spotted leaving the Cummins exhaust pipe. Newburn Bridge and the docks apart, the hardest point in the haul must have been the actual leaving of the factory. This, and all other 90-degree turns, saw the big driving wheels dig in and push hard, trying to straighten out the front wheels which had to scrabble hard to hold directional stability. Mainsforth Terrace in Hartlepool was closed to traffic when the load took up residence. At nearly 40 tonnes a row or over 3 tonnes a tyre, the negotiation of the Church Street railway crossing was very delicate and had to be timed for the early hours when there was a lack of opposing traffic.

The Contractor was a good tool, make no mistake about it. The steering lock could have been better and when running empty it was a bit leisurely, but for pulling the weights it was hard to beat for strength. Scammell knew they had a winner and there were numerous examples about to show that they were not a nine-day wonder and would last as long as you wanted. December 1977 saw Magnaload haul what was then the heaviest load ever pulled on

UK roads. At 401 tonnes, the 121 ft long moisture separator-reheater vessel was one of four similar loads made by GEC Larne bound for the San Onofre nuclear power station in California. For the haul to Belfast docks, the 16 rows of Scheuerle bogies were hauled by TRL 924H, the second-hand Magnaload Scammell, ably assisted by XUP 999F, which had been hired for the trip. This latter Contractor had started life with Siddle Cooks of Consett but, come the takeover, had eventually ended up with Northern Ireland Carriers, an offshoot to the Pickford empire. The two old tractors thought nothing of the 25-mile journey even though the all-up weight was 635 tonnes. Pickfords expect, and get, a long life from their fleet of Scammells and show little respect for their age. When they moved 730 tonnes in three lots from Immingham docks to Lindsey oil refinery at South Killingholme during the summer of 1978, the most impressive load must have been a 370-ton column which was over 40 ft high and 120 ft long. A National Coal Board conveyor had to be raised 21 ft to allow it to pass and there were 42 lamposts removed en route, by workmen not by the load. Pulling this vessel and the Nicholas running gear was SYO 384F, certainly ageing but not aged.

Prior to the Mammoet arrangement, the biggest tractor in the Econofreight fleet was UVN 44S. This well turned out Scammell worked hard for its living but very few people knew that it had already spent one lifetime working for ICI in Cheshire. Sunters also rebuilt one of their first Contractors, TPY 675H, after eight years of work. At a cost of £42,000 it shows the job was not skimped in any way, but it also shows what an operator will do rather than pay what he feels is Scammell's rather high price for a new one. The manufacturer may not have to worry a great deal when an operator is wanting a tractor to move over 200 tonnes for he is close to running a monopoly, but when the weight comes down a bit quite a few people, rather than go to Watford for their machines, have pulled out some interesting vehicles, most interesting of which must be the Searson alternative.

As one of the new generation of heavy hauliers, Peter Searson, MD of Heanor Haulage, just would not accept it when he could not get his ideal choice of tractor either because the manufacturer could not or would not build what he wanted. He did not particularly like the big Cummins engine nor did he want the semi-automatic transmission but when the conformists said there was no alternative he decided to show them there was. His reply was ONN 686P, an eight-wheeled tractive unit which looked a bit like a Volvo, a bit like a Scammell but was really a Heanor Haulage built HHT. The heart of the vehicle was a Detroit 8V92 engine pushing out 400 bhp and, to anyone who appreciated the sound of the old Foden two-stroke, it made a noise like Mozart. A special engine powered through a special 15-speed Fuller gearbox, via a Spicer clutch to an interesting rear bogie. Three Leyland axles were used to take a heavy loading from the semi-trailer but, in order to assist with manoeuvring, the foremost axle was not driven and could be lifted hobo style. To top it off a Volvo F88 sleeper-type cab was utilised which meant that with the engine compartment being outside up-ahead, there was ample room inside.

HHT 2 soon followed, although this one was of conventional 6 × 4 configuration whilst a splitter box was fitted offering over half a century of gear ratios. With plans to have five of these machines in his fleet, Peter Searson has no intention of putting Scammell out of business but the HHT's have already acquired a reputation of being able to pull the weight as well as being able to traverse the ground at a rapid pace.

Peter Sunter also came up with an alternative when he was searching for something to fill a gap in the North Yorkshire fleet. Scania and Volvo were already well represented and four Contractors formed Sunters' backbone but the outfit which took to the road in June 1978 was something entirely different. VVN 910S was its number and nearly everyone referred to it as a Mercedes as it passed rapidly by. Well it did have a Merc cab, a three-pointed star on the front plus a lot of Benz bits, but its true maker was Titan GmbH of Appenweier, West Germany. The making of the Titan was prompted by one Heinrich Schutz who was probably the German equivalent of Peter Searson. He, too, was frustrated when he could not get the heavy haulage tractors he wanted, so he approached Titan Special Purpose Vehicles Ltd who made things like fire engines and forestry vehicles. The result of this get-together was the Titan tractor but, unlike the HHT, there have been over a hundred of these produced and sold. Sunters' Titan I was a 6 × 4 version powered by the 21-litre Mercedes OM402 V12 engine, unturbocharged but still producing 420 bhp. Torque was 1,036 ft/lb at 1,600 rpm but the big thing it had was a ZF transmatic transmission. The eight-speed plus crawler synchromesh gearbox was driven through a WSK 400 torque converter so it meant all the power on tap could be put through the wheels and traction was assured. Lack of traction had been one of the consequences of the fluid flywheel of the SCG semi-automatic gearbox fitted to the Scammells. The Contractors suffered at times as not enough power could be transmitted when working at low revs, whereas the Titan would just walk away from a situation on tick-over with the torque converter multiplying the power up as required. The Titan was rated to run at up to 200 tonnes as an artic or 400 tonnes gross as a ballasted tractor whilst Ken Bickerton, its normal driver, regularly coaxed 80 on to the speedometer (km/h, of course) which reflects on the spread of performance which the vehicle could offer.

Titan II, EJW 229V, joined the Sunter fleet in February 1980. Nearly identical to its predecessor it did, however, sport a 6 × 6 configuration and was bought primarily as a ballasted tractor. Titan II's only 'fault' is being unable to get enough weight on to the front axle for, once this starts to spin, the outfit has to be stopped and all the diffs locked up before progress can be resumed. Cats-eyes, of all things, have a habit of knocking the axle into spin, so they are treated with great respect; not that restarting the vehicle is much of a worry as Malcolm Johnson found on the steep climb away from Penrith on the A66 near Stainton Village. More concerned with watching passing talent, he did not realise the Titan required a few more gears in hand and came to a gentle halt. There was 120 tonnes of concrete beam sitting on the back en route for Windscale but that made little difference and the outfit just eased away with the torque converter in full control.

Sunters' only question mark over the Titans is whether they will stay the pace as well as the Contractor but, of course, only time will tell. If they ever doubted that the vehicles could pull this was demonstrated at William Press's yard on Tyneside when Ken and Malcolm hitched the Titans up to 98 axles fitted with nearly 800 tyres supporting a production module destined for the Fulmar field. All-up weight was close to 2,400 tonnes and the two tractors moved it across site prior to being loaded-out. Yes, 2,400! The oil temperature gauges of the converters started to rise a bit but they were seen to be man enough for the job. Put the MkI Contractor on the open road where the throttle could be opened wide and it would probably out-pull the Titan, but on tick-over inching about a site, the torque converter nearly reigns supreme.

The Titans may have been different but they were at least recognisable which was something which could not be said about the next big loco-motive which came to Northallerton in 1981. If you had to guess you might say it was a Ford or Berliet and, in fairness, the cab was from Renault. The engine was the massive 450 Cummins, the whole machine being the product of Nicholas of France, the trailer maker, and went by the name of Tractormas. The beast is yet to prove itself but, with a Clark torque converter and gearbox in the

transmission line, its potential is very promising indeed.

The greatest user of home-produced tractors must have been Pickfords who, since the '50s, have shown a predominance of Scammell in their fleet. The National Freight Corporation were probably instrumental in the production of the Crusader for general haulage purposes and Pickfords, their heavy division, got good work from the stronger versions. 1970 saw an eight-wheeled artic tractor unit produced with the Motor Panels cab, Detroit engine and the name of Samson but only a handful of these were made. For 65 tonnes gross, the standard 6 × 4 Crusader was ideal but for 100-150 tonnes, Pickfords felt that use of the Contractor was an under-utilisation so, in search for something to fit, they went to MAN for their Jumbos. Versions of the 32.400 and 38.320 went into general service but when a 40.400 came over as a demonstrator in 1979, this was felt to be an even better machine and CYL 510V, an example fit for 180 tonnes based at Glasgow, is proof of the pudding.

Most favoured of the imports are undoubtedly the Swedish makes of Volvo and Scania, who have a great following in the lighter end of the business, not least with Mike Cave. Nine years after setting up shop in 1973 he has developed his one-man band into one of Europe's most respected heavy haulage companies. Based at Bedford, Planthaul Ltd specialises predominantly in overseas work travelling throughout the Common Market and as far afield as Egypt and Libya. Their immaculately turned out fleet is at present all Volvo, the flagships being three very special F12 6 × 4s, whilst the remainder consist of 13 assorted F12s and four F7 4 × 2s. With all the loads being driver-accompanied right through to their destination, the spares and service network maintained by Volvo in Europe is obviously a great attraction to a company in Planthaul's position. The trailers are also predominantly imports with Goldhofer and Broshius held in great esteem.

Planthaul operates solely artics but the SKPH ten-axle Goldhofer with hydraulic suspension, automatic steering and load compensation means that up to 140 tonnes can be carried without over-loading the king-pin or the tractors' drive axles. The latter is a problem which faces all heavy hauliers, the modern trend being wherever possible away from tractors and drawbar trailers which carry a heavy penalty of ballast. The sophisticated hydraulically suspended modular semi-trailer where axles can be added to order is ideal if the weight can be placed over these wheels, but for longer, awkward loads it may be impossible to keep the king-pin loading down to an acceptable level.

Low-loader operators in some other countries utilise two swan necks on their heavy artics with the first step frame semi-trailer being very short and only intended as a means of getting two or three more axles under the load. But, with UK legislation preventing the adoption of such tactics, Robert Wynns was one company which was trying to come up with some bright idea that would produce the same result. They also wanted an outfit which could carry 100-110-tonne loads but which would not exceed the magic figure of 152 tonnes gross taking them into special order work meaning greater Ministry control and expensive ship utilisation.

Sam Anderson went to Nicholas of France in 1978 with this problem and he returned with a design for a 150-tonne artic. The semi-trailer had two sets of axles mounted immediately behind the adjustable swan neck and before the commencement of the bed, whilst the remaining four rows followed at the end of the trailer. Automatic steering of all axles saw the front two rows steer in sympathy with the front axle of the drawing tractor whilst the back four turned in the opposite direction. This meant the turning circle of the outfit was relatively small as it seemed to handle more like a small rigid than a big artic, something the drivers had to remember at all times. The new concept answered the original questions although it did have its fair share of teething troubles, especially over the steering of the first two axles and adjustment of the weight distribution through the swan neck. Pickfords' Glasgow depot put one to work behind one of their big Jumbos whilst Dawsons of Middlesbrough used a bonneted Scania to haul theirs. Brackmills bought one, as did Heanor Haulage, but the latter were soon to sell theirs to G.C.S. Johnson, an up and coming heavy haulier operating an all-Scania fleet from Barton near Scotch Corner. Wynns had the largest tractor of the lot hauling their new semi in *Renown*, a large cabbed MkI Contractor modified slightly with suitable tyre equipment, based at Manchester.

The Wynns heavy haulage fleet of the early '80s had seen a big change from that of 25 years earlier with the imported heavy tractor now being the exception rather than the rule as the fleet was predominantly Scammell. Bedfords were used for the lighter loads whilst Wynns had a version of the 6 × 4 Crusader called *Amazon* which was fit for 100 tonnes gross operation. Both light and heavy versions of the Contractor were utilised and Wynns were probably the only UK operator to use these big Scammells generally in articulated form. In fact in the Sudan, powerful *Hercules* regularly ran as a double bottom, an artic pulling a drawbar trailer. Wynns had not got into the heavy load-out field as

much as Sunters, although utilising these techniques they had regularly moved anything up to 500 tonnes from or on to adjacent shipping. They did not have the great demand for torque converters on their tractors but, when Scammell offered this option on the MkII Contractors with the bigger 450 Cummins engine, *Invincible* and *Superior* came to enhance the fleet with this specification.

Wynns were reckoned to have been involved in practically every heavy engineering exercise in Wales since the late 19th century, the most unusual of which must have been the construction of the CEGB Dinorwic pumped storage station inside the Elidir mountain, Llanberis, North Wales. The scheme puts into use two lakes, one at the top of the mountain and one towards the bottom. When power is needed, the tap is turned on and the top lake releases water which is channelled through tubing to the bottom lake and generates electricity by driving turbines in a similar manner to that by which numerous hydro-electric schemes operate. To ensure Dinorwic never runs out of water, during the night on cheap rate electricity the contents of the bottom lake are pumped back up to the top ready to supply instant power once more to the national grid as and when the requirement is made. What will probably most please environmentalists is that when the scheme is completed there will be very little to damage the beauty of Snowdonia, as everything is concealed inside the mountain.

Chris Millers of Preston were involved in moving lots of the turbine equipment from the manufacturers, Markhams of Chesterfield, to site but, such was the geography of North Wales, that most of the traffic had to be hauled between Manchester and Port Penryn by ship. Amongst the heaviest loads were six valves used to control the flow of water out of the top lake and, at 150 tonnes each, they must have been some of the heaviest taps ever made. To suit these big taps, Millers operated what was believed to be one of the biggest Macks in the world, a 6 × 4 ballasted tractor rated for 240 tonnes gross operation. The Bulldog made the greatest impact of all the American trucks in the UK market of the late '70s with quite a number finding their way into heavy haulage operations. The maxidyne engine was renowned for its pulling ability and general haulage versions rarely had anything more than a five-speed gearbox such was the spread of performance that the flexible engine could offer but, to ensure it lived up to its rating, Millers' Mack had 12 gears in its transmission line. The loads were carried by Cometto modular running gear, ten rows and a set of girders utilised to carry the 14 ft wide valves. Millers made great use of the hydraulic suspension on the Italian trailers for picking up and depositing their charges, an asset also greatly appreciated by one heavy engineering company turned haulier.

Whessoes of Darlington were contracted to produce 4,600 tonnes of steel pipes ranging from 8 ft 6 ins to 14 ft 9 ins in diameter and in sections weighing up to 130 tonnes, for installation inside the mountain. Transportation from County Durham to North Wales was put in the capable hands of Sunters and the Fisher boats but actually to place the linings in position, Whessoes bought one special outfit and did it themselves. The locomotive part of the combination was XDC 485S, a Contractor, but with 32 tonnes of ballast on its back it tipped the scales at 50 tonnes gross. The special trailers were two Cometto model 52M units, each having five axles and a special curved bed both to accept the round pipes but, more importantly, to keep the load as low as possible for passage through the internal tunnels where clearance at times was only 1 ft 8 ins. The dished construction meant that each axle could only be fitted with two pairs of small tyres but their carrying capacity was still 13 tonnes per line provided a speed limit of 3 mph was observed. Inching around the inside of the mountain where gradients on wet slate were as steep as 1 in 8 in places meant that there was little likelihood of the outfit being able to go faster than a walking pace, so the speed restriction was irrelevant. For the lighter pipes the trailers were used individually but for the heaviest sections which were as long as 75 ft, the trailers were joined up as a 48 ft long ten row pulled by a 19 ft 6 ins long drawbar to overcome the fore and aft load overhangs. The high manoeuvreability through all-wheel steering, plus the electro-hydraulic suspension of the trailers were crucial features of getting the linings into position. The Scammell may have done all the pushing and pulling, but the steering of the trailer was done manually through the use of a 'wander lead' plugged into the hydraulic control panel. At the point of installation the suspension was activated to raise the load 1 ft 2 ins where it was supported on jacks to leave it clear of the trailer bed as the hydraulics were lowered and the trailer withdrawn.

Whessoe were pleased with the performance of the combination as were Crane Fruehauf who were distributing the Cometto in the UK. The market was getting congested with numerous different brands of modular trailer but manufacturers realised that once a haulier opted for a particular type he was more than likely to re-order with that make to ensure continuity. There were exceptions, of course, with Econofreight using Nicholas yet inheriting Scheuerle when they merged with Magnaload-Mammoet. Pickfords also operated a mixture of modular gear but Heanor Haulage and Wrekin Roadways were two companies which had opted away from the popular Nicholas and gone for Cometto. Both were to operate examples of the 14-row girder trailer to haul concentrated loads, Wrekins' version, purchased in 1975 having a capacity of 250 tons. This company had literally stepped up a notch in the mid-'70s because being based at Telford made them ideally placed to compete for the heavy electrical traffic out of the Midlands which had so long been the domain of either Pickfords or Wynns. Such was the success of Wrekins that, in 1979, they were bought out by the Bulwark Group to join forces with Sunters and Wynns rather than fight against them. Following group policy, Wrekins transferred their preference to Nicholas running gear and as the Cometto went to Hong Kong, Britain's biggest transporter joined the Shropshire fleet. 20 rows of axles supported the 310-ton capacity girders and, with a price tag of more than £600,000, it was expected to be one of the best trailers in the world. But during its maiden journey in May 1980, whilst carrying a 258-ton GEC generator from Stafford to Manchester, cracks appeared in the trailer chassis resulting in a rather premature stoppage. These may have been rectifiable, but it did bring home that, even with the best of equipment, heavy haulage is a business which is always full of surprises.

The new 20-row Nicholas may have brought axle loadings down to around the 20 tonnes mark without the need for the air cushion equipment, but with the overall length of the outfit being 245 ft it did mean that, even with all wheel steering, there were numerous road situations which could not be negotiated. Getting in and out of customers' premises was also sometimes impossible with this type of trailer so, when conditions dictated, it was back to the old 12-row and the hoverlift, although ACE 2 had now replaced ACE 1. Gone was the blower truck which hooked up behind substituting for one of the locomotives and in its place, mounted on the back of the girder trailer, was a self-contained unit consisting of four gas turbine engines which could produce a greater cushion relief in a more efficient manner than the old system. Wrekins, Wynns and Pickfords trailers which used the ACE 2 were all fitted with suitable brackets to accept the engines, so switching the new equipment from one haulier to another was also not much of a problem.

As mentioned earlier, both Wynns and Pickfords had encountered situations where bridges had become so weakened that, even with the air cushion equipment working at full thrust, there was still a great likelihood of something like the incidents at Boroughbridge and Ardrossan occurring again.

Normally routes like this were avoided like the plague but where there was no alternative then the haulier had to improvise. The CEGB had amongst its diverse equipment a large steel construction which was used for numerous things but was mainly intended as a loading ramp for getting on and off coastal shipping. The innovative haulier's use of this ramp was to place it just above, but completely clear of, the suspect roadway completely bridging the bridge so that the outfit was able to drive across the weak bridge yet at no time touch it.

Mammoet-Econofreight needed more than the CEGB loading ramp when they delivered what was then the largest load ever moved on the roads of the UK and, had it not been for a particular wedding in July 1981 coinciding with the move, then a lot more publicity would have no doubt been attracted to it. Being able to offer a complete packaged delivery operation right from the manufacturer in Holland to its destination at the PV3 lube plant in Esso's Fawley refinery, Mammoet-Econofreight were one of the few hauliers which could be seriously considered to haul the 476-tonne, 193 ft 9 ins long, 42 ft 4 ins high distillation column. The journey commenced with the SIF vessel being lifted by crane on to a barge which took it down the canals to Rotterdam. To cross the North Sea and the English Channel, the barge was floated on to a very special ship belonging to the Mammoet fleet. Looking like a cross between a deep-sea tug and a floating dry dock, the boat was constructed so that the rear part hinged open allowing the carrying part to be flooded, thus permitting smaller vessels just to float in as though they were being swallowed up by a whale. Once the sea journey was completed, the barge was disgorged and, with no suitable dock facilities available which could handle this enormous load, the sea-going mount was simply beached on the shore line adjacent to the Fawley CEGB power station. If getting the load back on to dry land was delicate, reaching the actual surfaced roads was just plain hard work. To negotiate the 440-yard stretch of hardcore, Econofreight had constructed a 28 ft wide roadway made up of 12 in by 12 in timbers. 125 yards were laid then, as the load passed over it, the vacated timbers were moved to the front in leap-frog fashion in a move which went like clockwork. On to the roadway things were relatively straightforward although, to surmount an incline inside the power station complex, four tractors were hitched up to ensure traction on the greasy road surface. On to the public roads the two leading Scammells were uncoupled and the 5-mile haul to the refinery was completed using TRL 924H, that ageing ex-Magnaload Contractor, and underlining the Dutch presence, a

6 × 4 FTF of the Mammoet fleet. Entering the Esso refinery should have been a time when everyone was to breathe a sigh of relief but devising a method to manoeuvre the beast round the internal installations was the point where UK project manager, Toby Allin, had to work for his living. There was no way the outfit could turn the required 90-degree turn in the space available, so an AK680 mobile crane was used to lift first the front and then the rear of the vessel whilst the bogies were manoeuvred into position round the corner ensuring the remainder of the haul was just a formality.

The early '80s saw recession hit the haulage industry causing a lot of operators to tighten their belts and prune their overheads. Wrekin Roadways were to disappear as they merged with Wynns Heavy Haulage, although 1982 saw the newly-named Pickfords Industrial pass out of government ownership as the NFC became a publicly-owned company. The prospects for heavy haulage are still very exciting and closing this history with an account of a very special move, leads me to believe that whenever there are loads to be carried, there will always be men and machines able to haul the heavyweights.

This well turned out Scania belonging to Dawsons of Middlesbrough is seen on a pre-operational test run, in August 1980, running at a gross combination weight of 120 tons. This configuration of Nicholas axles combined to a gooseneck which can be adjusted to vary the imposed tractor weight must be ideal for opeators who prefer to use artics to their maximum permitted 150 tons under the Special Types General Order.

Right Peter Clemmett and *Fearnought* are seen late in January 1979 with this waste heat boiler destined for the oil terminal at Sullom Voe. The automatically steered ten row vehicle is tracking well, whilst Sunters' Titan I in articulated form is seen in convoy waiting for progress to be recommenced.

Right One of the first MAN Jumbo 150-tonners seen in this country was this 40.400 which came over as a demonstrator in the summer of 1979. Pickfords had use of it for some time as did British Nuclear Fuels, but it is seen here being used by Heanor Haulage with a Blackwood Hodge caterpillar on a King tri-axle semi-trailer en route from Hartlepool to the South Coast.

Below Econofreight of Teeside are seen hauling this 110 ft long air separation plant from Edmonton, North London, to Tilbury prior to export to Africa late in 1979. All up weight was about 110 tons, well within the 180-ton capacity of the Fiat 300 PT, a rare tractor in UK heavy haulage. The hydraulic suspension of the Nicholas bogies were put to good use in loading and unloading, an asset appreciated by lots of other operators.

Left Sunters' Titan I eases over Newport Bridge, Middlesbrough, in October 1980 with one of three silver vessels in convoy manufactured by Head Wrightsons for BP Chemicals. Bound for the docks at Hartlepool, this 170 ft long 'cigar' weighed in at 130 tonnes. Ro-ro'd up to Grangemouth, the vessels were part of the No 3 ethanol plant being constructed by Davy McKee.

Below Since the opening of Foster Wheeler Power Products in 1968, Seaton Carew has seen its fair share of abnormal load traffic, however this Sunter quartet seen on July 29 1979 must rank as the biggest convoy yet. Bill Jamieson leads with a package boiler at about 250 tons destined for Hartlepool whilst his three colleagues had a further 20 miles with their charges bound for distant Teesport.

Keeping a good lookout for low flying aircraft, Wrekins moved this 85 ft long, 125-ton pedestrian walkway in October 1980 from Terminal 1 to Terminal 2 at Gatwick airport, utilising a pair of Cometto three-axle bogies.

April 1978 saw Malcolm Johnson ease his F89 back on to dry land prior to hauling these Whesshoe lining pipes up to the new Dinorwic power station, North Wales.

Miller's mighty Mack *Bonzo Bear* takes time out from trekking up to Dinorwic to deliver this 150-ton piece of electrical equipment in the London area.

Hauling this 130-ton paper drum from South Shields to Prudhoe in early 1981, Mammoet-Econofreight covered a distance as the crow flies of no more than 15 miles. But with height and weight limits combined with ice and snow playing havoc with the route, the F89-Contractor-Scheuerle outfit took ten days to complete the haul.

Bill Jamieson rounds Churchyard roundabout in Stockton early in 1981 with this 129 tonnes vessel to be ro-ro'd out to sunnier climes. Sunters do not wish to talk too much about this load for on its first journey to the docks it fell off the trailer and had to be returned to the makers for scrutiny.

Below Although having worked hard for most of its life at the ICI salt mines in Cheshire, Econofreight still expect and get a lot from this rejuvenated Contractor. It is seen close to the end of a short haul into ICI Wilton with this impressive 104-ton vessel early in 1981.

This page Sunters Titan II, their Tractormas and two of the Contractors plus 44 rows of Nicholas running gear were needed to haul 708 tons of impressive Head Wrightson vessels. The four loads were hauled from Thornaby to Hartlepool docks in June 1982 prior to their sea journey to the USSR.

The two ex-Magnaload Volvos shepherd this accommodation module across the dock side prior to its being loaded out at Lowestoft in July 1981. At 550 tons it would be described as fairly small, it being one of four similar loads bound for the Maureen field.

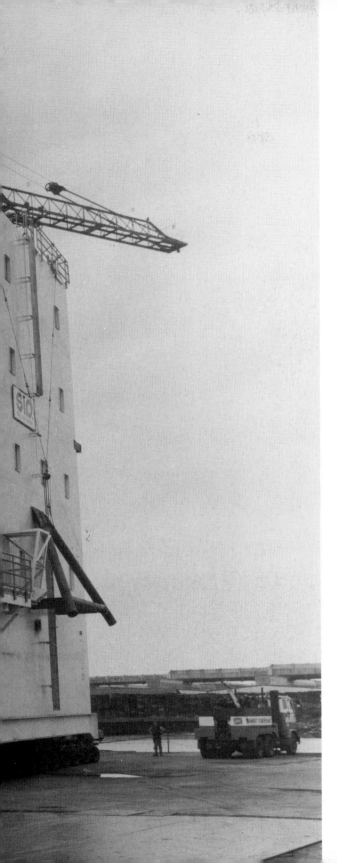

Above Two of the immaculate fleet of Planthaul of Bedford having just returned from Poland with two heavy castings destined for Leeds. These were no problem to the F12-Goldhofer combinations.

Below The gas project being constructed at Mossmorran, Southern Scotland in late 1982 brought lots of work for Mammoet-Econofreight and also gave the exciting new Scammell an opportunity to show its paces. Driver Ernie Pickersgill missed his normal Volvo N10 but he couldn't fault the S24 for sheer strength, yet even he was taken aback when the manufacturer's engineers asked him to stop the outfit on a 1 in 10 incline at an all up weight of 286 tons and then restart it. The big 350 Cummins and Brockhouse torque converter driving through Spicer gearbox and Michelin sand type tyres didn't even sigh and moved off as if they were on the flat.

Left The N10 is not a common machine in UK heavy haulage, although Econofreight find that the fitting of a torque converter more than compensates for the lack of power in the 290 engine. The Volvo-Nicholas combination is seen on a short haul across Cleveland in March 1982, all up weight 116 tons, overall length 143 ft.

Below Mammoet-Econofreight hauling in July 1981 what was then the heaviest load moved on roads in the UK. At 476 tonnes, 193 ft 9 ins long and 42 ft 4 ins high, the vessel needed four tractors to ensure traction up this incline on the private roads inside the Fawley power station. The 5-mile road haul was completed using the ex-Magnaload Contractor and an FTF of the Mammoet fleet.

Right Although this enormous monster was termed a mobile crane, when it came to moving from one end of the Port of London to another it was far more efficient to use a heavy haulier. Mammoet-Econo-freight used ten rows of Nicholas running gear plus two of their strongest Volvos as a prerequisite of the all up weight being in excess of 350 tons.

Below Coming to the Sunter fleet in late 1981 was this French-built Tractormas. One of its first road hauls was the carriage of this 120-ton Head Wrightson kiln section from Thornaby to Avonmouth in May 1982.

BRITISH MACHINERY FOR AYLESFORD PAPER MILLS

ALBERT E REED & CO — KENT

ED. BOX & Co., Ltd.

KD-9168

175

EDWARD BOX & Co. Ltd. Incorporating M.R.S. Ltd
LIGHTBODY STREET, LIVERPOOL
Depots at LONDON, BIRMINGHAM, MANCHESTER, SHEFFIELD & GLASGOW

35. PAPER DRYING CYLINDER. 14 ft 1 in. DIAM
60 TONS   BURY TO AYLESFORD

PICKFORDS

7. The 100-ton club is formed

With the current membership of this club increasing day by day it seems hard to believe that it was only formed in 1929 and then by just a single member. Membership doubled within a couple of years but the club then stayed stagnant for close on two decades. It was the demands of industry in the 1950s and '60s which made the numbers increase swiftly and, although this book is intended as a review of some of the current members only, a sense of reverence and nostalgia dictates that we look back and admire some of those early founders.

The criterion laid down for joining was very simple: it was the ability to haul a genuine 100 tons of payload or, in other words, to be rated to operate at least at 150 tons gross train weight operation. Nowadays such a haul may seem beneath contempt to members of the Super Club who think nothing of pulling 1,000 tons, but for KD9168 and BLH21, the magic 100 was their passport to never ending fame. To these two old girls this was a milestone which was passed not with ease but with a lot of suffering inflicted not only on their hard-working crews but also on any stretch of road which had to support them through their unyielding solid rubber tyres. Even when they were 20 years old the two old girls were still working for their keep, but in the '50s the two founders were allowed to hand in their membership cards and retire gracefully as new trucks came forward to take their place. Current members boast anything between 300-500 bhp from their big

modern diesel engines and, although some of us may laugh at the paltry 86 bhp which the two early vehicles had on tap from the Scammell petrol engines, we should really lift our hats in salute.

There was certainly no shortage of 100-ton loads even in the early days. Certainly there was enough work to keep Pickfords, Norman E. Box, Wynns and Rudds very busy. However, it was necessary in those days for the haulier to double, triple or quadruple his assortment of tractors to haul this heavy traffic.

One famous American truck made a great contribution to heavy haulage but, with due respect to the Pacific Car and Foundry Company, it should be remembered that Wynns had done the development work which made the tractor such a success. Their first Hercules engine pushed out 176 bhp, which gave the drivers' mate a lot more peace of mind. When working on previous, underpowered machines, every steep hill had seen him leave his hot seat for an even hotter seat on the tractor's front mudguard. For, with the bonnet up and a piece of stick in his hand, he could force back the fuel pump governor to produce more power for the driver, although this procedure was known to produce a rather anti-social smokescreen.

The old-fashioned chain drive did mean a lot of shocks could be absorbed in the elasticity of the transmission but every steep incline meant a lengthy halt at the bottom while the crew had to change to a smaller drive sprocket manually. It was heaven indeed when Foden solved this problem in their specials by using hand-operated reduction hubs, but if the mate forgot to turn one out of the four levers then 'ping!' — the half-shaft would snap just like that.

PPY264 was Sunters' sturdy Foden 100-tonner and, although her power was increased with the use of the eight-cylinder Gardner engine, she was still painfully slow. To break the monotony whilst going up steep inclines like Stanedge, between Hudders-

Above left Member 1 of the 100-ton club was KD9168. Reproduced from some publicity material of Edward Box & Co, this shot shows the vehicle in 1936 hauling a very impressive cylinder from Bury to Aylesford. **Left** BLH21 was originally built as a 65 tonner but later uprating in her capacity meant she became member 2 of the select club. 'Leaping Lena', as she was known, is seen in the works of Vickers Armstrongs, Newcastle, in about 1947, proving her claim to fame as she hauls part of a car press and also shows off her sophisticated air-conditioning system!

field and Oldham, the mate would jump out of the cab, walk up ahead and still have time to sunbathe as the 6 × 4 shuffled its way ever leisurely upwards.

The arrival of the Rolls-Royce-powered Constructor shattered this tranquillity when it joined the 100-ton club. Those who disbelieve that the two-levered, 12-geared 6 × 6 met the requirement of strength for membership should talk to Siddle Cook who proved the model's qualifications beyond doubt. However, his 14-year-old son thought the monster was more like a big dinky car when he regularly romped round the Consett yard behind the wheel, although he virtually had to stand on the seat to see out of the small windscreen. For those who wanted even more strength, Scammell introduced the Super Constructor and, were it not for the odd special from people like Rotinoff, then club membership lists would have seemed rather repetitive in the types of make at work.

There is no place for the Diamond T in the hall of fame. These machines were only rated at 85 tons gtw although Sunter's veteran driver, Jimmy Goulding, would tell you he regularly pulled loads of over 100 tons with his Crook & Willington

Carriers' 'T'. The transmission of the vehicle naturally rebelled at this abuse, sometimes with amusing results. Battle tanks were a regular cargo during the '50s as they were hauled from ordnance depots to scrap yards prior to burning up. The Hercules engine was giving its best as Jim's outfit clawed its way up a testing hill one day, although a farmer in an adjacent field wasn't really concerned as he was concentrating on ploughing his furrows straight. All were taken by surprise when, with an almighty crack, the half-shaft finally snapped and shot out sideways, straight through the hedge and missed the farmer by inches. Convinced the tank was shooting at him and hostilities had recommenced, he forsook his ploughing and was last seen disappearing down the hillside as fast as his little legs would go. It took the assistance of two petrol-engined Antars before the hill was cleared, although no record was kept on how long the field remained unploughed. But enough of days gone by, this book is intended as a look at current club members starting off with a model which some believe to be leader of the pack.

When the extra-heavy loads came along, people like Pickfords had to make multiple use of their tractors as is shown here, where four Diamond Ts were required to move this 185-ton casting. The outfit is seen in Sheffield about 1955 with the quoted gross weight of 245 tons being slightly wrong. The six-axle Crane girder-trailer was nearer 80 tons than 60 tons unladen and, along with the tractors, all-up combination weight would be close to 400 tons.

Wynns wonder wagons, the mighty Pacifics, proved to be of great service to their company. Wynns also made extensive use of the various Crane girder trailers with two different models, fleet numbers 567 and 789 on show. Both the outfits are seen about 1965, with 'Challenger' on Breeze Hill near Southport roundabout at Bootle, while 'Dreadnought', with 'Valiant' pushing, is en route to Monk Fryston near Selby, with 213 tons on the back of its 300-ton capacity trailer.

Left The biggest dinky car in Consett was Siddle Cook's SPT 600, or so the son of the owner, Raymond Cook thought. The Constructor is seen working for its living on the A1 near Scotch Corner, in about 1964, with an NCB locomotive being hauled from a colliery works in north-west Durham on its way to an overhaul.

Below Bradwell was the first and perhaps the biggest job that Sunters' Rotinoff was involved with in the score of years that she worked for that company. The first of 12 238-ton boilers is seen in May 1958 dwarfing all it passes, as it makes its steady way to the power-station.

Above Sunters' PPY264 was their distinctive version of the Foden 100-ton capacity tractor. The massive grille was required to cool its eight-cylinder Gardner engine, which created sauna-type working conditions inside the crew cab. She is seen leaving Wolviston in 1964 on the A19, making her leisurely way to Sunderland with a Head Wrightson load being supported on the Crane 60-ton capacity float-trailer.

Right Photographer Alan Simpson recorded plenty of police attention for Sunters' first Super Constructor 447 DPY as she approached the Five Lamps at Thornaby on December 20 1968. The Head Wrightson vessel was en route to ICI Wilton on south Teesside. The solid-tyred Crane bogies are seen in use; Sunters got 19 hard years of work out of them before their enforced retirement in 1976. They and their Rotinoff were subsequently donated to the Transport Museum at Swindon.

8. The Contractor is club captain

For close on 20 years the Scammell Contractor has been the favoured motive power for the vast majority of the big UK heavy-haulage operators. Pickfords naturally adopted them as they had used nearly all the Scammell range since the days of 'Leaping Lena' but Wynns, too, were ready to trade in their Pacifics and Diamond Ts and accept the latest Watford models. Most of the early purchases have long since gone out to grass, although the first Contractor bought by Sunters is still making a big contribution in their fleet's workload. The Northallerton company had been slow to take this model for, even as late as 1967, they had preferred to buy KVN860E, the all-wheel drive 6×6 Super Constructor, which gave better performance off the road than the 6×4 Contractor. But as the '70s approached a new fleet flagship was an obvious necessity and TPY675H became the first Contractor to arrive at Boroughbridge Road.

Powering this Scammell was the 14-litre Cummins engine pushing out 335 bhp at 2,100 rpm, the middle one of the three Cummins engine options available to the standard Rolls-Royce Eagle 300. The transmission was the Self-Changing Gears RV30, eight forward, two reverse semi-automatic gearbox which, when used with a fluid coupling, is simplicity itself to operate. There is no clutch pedal to worry about; changing gear is just a matter of pulling or pushing on a stubby little lever which bounces back to the vertical position once hand pressure is released. The driver does not even have to know what gear he is in, although there is an illuminated indicator, for all up and down changes are made in the same direction and it is impossible to miss a gear. There tends to be a jerk through the transmission with a change but this can be eased by simultaneously grading the use of the accelerator. Driver No 1 of fleet No 175 was John Robinson, the undisputed senior chauffeur of the depot with 40 years experience at the company — a man well used to the idiosyncracies of this type of transmission.

An early haul for John and the Contractor involved taking an impressive 25 ft diameter Kaldo vessel from Whessoe, Darlington, to Consett Iron Company. The steel works is in the midst of a circuit of low bridges so that it seemed, at first, as if anything over 20 ft high could not get through. Henry Wood, then operations manager, had a bright idea. They went up the A68 to Castleside, a route which took the Scammell-Crane combination right through Moorside and up through the Grove. Virtually a stone's throw away from the works, but with a low bridge in the way, the load turned left back down through a housing estate. A narrow stretch of high-walled road forced a detour through someone's back garden and then they had to get down the 1 in 5 Mutton Clog bank towards Allensford with the brakes screaming. Peter Clemmett in KVN860E was leading with John and the Contractor hanging on at the rear and, hard though it may be to believe, the combination of weight and incline then made the outfit unstoppable. Both drivers put everything on but the 200 tons just inched on and on. It would not go any faster than two or three mph but it would not go any slower. A 12 ins $\times$ 12 ins timber sleeper was thrown in front of the trailer but it simple ran over it and still would not stop. In fact nothing at all would stop the load trickling down the incline. You have to have strong nerves in this business but everyone started to breathe a lot easier as the right-hander at the bottom was negotiated and the road pointed upwards. Bridgehill and Blackhill are like mountain sides but as the Scammells were going up and not down they were relatively straightforward. The destination was reached without further incident, although perhaps there were a few more grey hairs above Henry Wood's spectacles.

With John Robinson promoted to route-finding and job-checking, the keys of the Contractor were handed over to Jimmy Goulding, at that time a slip of a lad at 52 years. Jimmy, or Gino to his friends, a nickname which followed him from his war years in Italy, had seen practically everything in haulage, but the early '70s saw him and Sunters enter an entirely new phase in moving. With the North Sea oil boom came massive load-outs and site moves of things which dwarfed even the massive Scammell. Laings wanted one of the 'Teeside Twins' to be moved on site at Graythorpe and when John Garrett clambered to the top of this massive site crane, there was only 6 ins left on the 100 ft tape when he dropped it down. Peter Sunter was considering taking the crane to pieces but Jimmy and John had different ideas. Utilising SB3, the six-axle Crane girder trailer, they slipped under the crane, packed up with timbers then gently activated the internal hydraulics which picked up trailer, timbers and crane, the latter just an inch or two off the ground. With the Contractor in first gear it was eased over the site with only gravity holding it in place. After all, it could only have fallen an inch or two but it did not even do that as the smooth running Scammell proved to its boss just what it could do.

Moving the 50 ft square base plate was slightly different and required the use of four bogies, one at each of the corners. Balancing something like this is always a lot harder than, say, carrying it supported at two or three points and as the two pushing tractors eased the load down a steep incline, the load lifted off one of the bogies allowing it to slip itself out

of position. The tractors were stopped and although the spring parking brake on the Contractor held it firm, the multi-pull brake on the Rotinoff was not as sure. Its driver, Peter Clemmett, had dismounted to assist with the bogie and thus he was helpless when the tractor started to inch forward slewing the base plate round. Lol Johnson was the first to spot the danger and went to shout, 'Stop the wagon!' But, in his excitement, all he succeeded in doing was to spit out his false teeth which disappeared into the darkness. The Rotinoff was halted without any damage but then everyone had to turn to and grope around underneath the bogie to find Lol's molars.

What makes TPY675H different from many other Contractors is apparent from what happened during the six months following February 2 1978. After more than seven hard years the Scammell was starting to fray at the edges. As the only suitable replacement was an identical, rather expensive Mark 1 Contractor, Peter Sunter thought it might be possible to rebuild the original machine. So after carefully costing the exercise, that is exactly what Sunters engineers did. Under the guidance of Roy Pickard, Ted Beasley and Bob Lincoln first stripped off everything that would come off, apart from the cab. Moving thousands of tons had taken its toll on the engine and gearbox, which were sent off for refurbishing, but not even the closest of examinations could reveal any faults in the Contractor's chassis or in its massive back bogie. Over two

This wasn't Sunters' first excursion to the rain forests of deepest Indonesia, but it does give some indication of the tortuous route that this Whessoe vessel had to follow to get to Consett Iron Company. Photographer Arthur Philipson spotted the outfit as it had to detour through someone's back garden in order to miss a narrow stretch of high-walled road.

months were spent on the mechanical side of the Scammell which included modifying the ballast box to incorporate a walk-round catwalk and improving the power-assisted steering to ease Gino's aching muscles. The vehicle then went off to Scarborough for the cab to be rebuilt in true coach fashion at Plaxtons. The Contractor which returned was no ordinary vehicle for even five years later its immaculate wood-panelled interior still puts some boardrooms to shame. The end product received acclaim even from Scammells. It also warranted a new registration so, as TPY675H disappeared into a heap of rejected rubble, YVN308T came back in its place.

Sunters were to operate four of the crew-cabbed Contractors but it was the big two, Pickfords and Wynns, who were the greatest UK purchasers of this Scammell model. Their unabashed rivalry continued, although now that they were using almost identical weapons it was a lot easier to compare their performance. The crews, of course, never knew when their progress was being observed.

Serving the electrical industry, even in far-flung parts of the country, kept both companies busy. Wynns had particularly strong links with the town of Penzance, which was the only suitable roll-off point in the area. Unfortunately, the haul back up to the Indian Queens sub-station, near Newquay, was a hard pull through the testing Cornwall countryside. Once the load was discharged, the empty ride back to base with the massive girder trailer was still no picnic as driver Roger Banfield found when he became stuck fast on a tight corner in the aptly named Buckfastleigh on the A38. All he had on the trailer were a few supporting timbers and a sheet, which looked something like a pea on a drum, but the trailer could not be reduced any further. Roger was surveying his predicament when one of the locals came up and said, 'Nay lad, that's no good'. Thinking the old man might be able to wave a magic wand and extricate him, Roger asked what he meant. 'Well' the local said, 'Pickfords came round here last week with a load twice the size you've got and they didn't have any trouble.' How do you answer that? You just have to get back into the cab and get on with it.

The standard crew cab is an airy if somewhat noisy place to work in. There is room to get up and stretch your legs, even make a brew on the stove or wash your hands in the wash basin. It is like a dance hall when compared to the small three-seater cab fitted on the lightweight version of the Contractor. Jack Hill of Botley was faced with this problem when he purchased TRL924H, 'Betsy' as she's now affectionately known, from Mid Cornwall

Contractors in 1972. Jack had bought it to haul his 200-ton-capacity Crane girder trailer about so, along with a ballast box, he added a D8 Caterpillar tractor cab to provide extra crew accommodation and sleeping quarters. However, even with this extra convenience the southern crew thought 'Betsy' was more of a beast and few of a the Hill men liked working on her. When in May 1976 she changed hands again and moved to a new company they did not miss her too much.

Magnaload of Billingham was a joint venture set up between Peckstons the shippers and Mammoet Transport BV of Amsterdam. Moving massive loads by winching, jacking or skidding was where this company was to shine, but road hauls were just as important. NPY439P was their first buy, a 180-ton capacity Volvo F89 ballast tractor, but a 240-ton Contractor was also a necessity for the weights which were to be hauled. Scammell would willingly fill the order for a new one provided Magnaload could wait 18 months, something which was clearly impossible. Second-hand Contractors were few and far between but it was found that 'Betsy' was available and, for the exchange of £18,000, she journeyed north to start work in earnest. She may have been pleased to leave Southampton but her hasty departure caused her to be booked for speeding on the A34 for doing a highly illegal 54 mph. The cramped timetable which was waiting for her on arrival meant that her modifications amounted to little more than a quick repaint and the removal of the sleeper cab. Even the 15 tons of ballast was poured in as liquid concrete which proved far easier to put in place than it was to remove.

It was at the William Press yard on Tyneside that the Contractor was first to show her potential when Magnaload loaded out the first of the really big North Sea oil modules. Moving it around the site up to the quayside there were supposed to be three lorry-based winches doing the pull but when the Volvo and FTF's mechanism malfunctioned, it was the lone Darlington winch on 'Betsy' that just kept pulling and pulling on its own. True she was well anchored down, but 2,400 tons was an impressive weight to winch about unassisted.

Later the same year 'Betsy' went to Norther Ireland to haul by road the first of four massive GEC vessels from Larne to Belfast, these being eventually destined for California. At 401 tonnes they were the heaviest loads to be moved in the UK and with the all-up weight of each outfit being well over 600 tonnes it meant that the two Magnaload locomotives required assistance. Protocol dictated an Ulster vehicle should be used but, though XUP999F headed up the roadtrain with 'Northern

Ireland Carriers' written on the door, historians knew its first owner was the late famous north-eastern haulier Siddle C. Cook. The police escort were accompanied by an army escort and both were followed by most of the province who had turned out to watch. The 5-mile climb away from the coast had the two Scammells panting hard but it was at the M2 motorway overbridge that highway engineers were waiting in a cold sweat. They had made their calculations but at this sort of weight things were still very theoretical. The pulling tractors were unhitched to ease the weight as much as possible and to get the load over the 150 ft span 'Betsy' winched it across whilst the ballasted Volvo controlled the movement by letting its winch out from the other side. The bridge sank two centimetres but, when the load reached the other side, the engineers gladly reported that it had bounced back to its correct position. The run down into Belfast was straightforward but with a haul time of 14 hours it meant the outfit had not quite managed two mph, but who was watching the clock? The only problem encountered by driver, Dave Ruffels, and the rest of the crew was finding somewhere suitable when nature called!

For the second load the sightseers did not turn up as they had seen it all before and for the third even the police escort forgot to appear. When load number four was to be moved the Magnaload tractors were wanted elsewhere, so it was up to the more modern Contractors of Wrekin Roadways to do the necessary for this one.

The late '70s was a hard time for the ageing Scammell. If she was not winching massive loads on site or hauling small mountains on the roads, she was running empty trailers from site to base or from base to site. A Dutch FTF was imported from Holland to help in the hauls but the main competition to be the champion vehicle of Magnaload came from the two 6 × 4 F89s. All three tractors worked very closely together but it was not until December 1979 that there was a direct head-to-head road haul to settle the argument once and for all.

Moving two 137-ton railway cranes from NEI Cowans Sheldon at Carlisle down to Workington docks, prior to export to New Zealand, proved quite an administrative headache for the routing staff. Twelve axles were put under each of the loads to bring the running weight down to 15 tons a line, but it still meant that the all-up weight was over 220 tons, which is heavy in anyone's book. The plan of the journey was agreed, 'Betsy' led with the first load whilst RAJ530R followed with the second. Once the Scammell had been forced to change down to second gear, a radio message was passed to the following Volvo so NPY439P could hook up and

double-head till the incline was cleared. A straight-forward idea but, of course, the best laid plans. . .

Anyone travelling the A595 from Carlisle to Cockermouth by car might be excused for not even noticing Bothel. The 2-mile climb probably would not warrant a change of gear on a clear road but to a heavy haulier Bothel is long and it just gets progressively steeper as the top is reached. This was one bank which was to find 'Betsy' having to drop down to second gear so, when a radio message for help was received by the following load, they stopped at the bottom, double-headed then set off up that fearsome incline. It was a hard pull for the Swedish duo but what they did not expect to see in the distance was 'Betsy' stationary on the steepest part of the hill. 'Crikey!' they thought, 'if she can't make it what will we do?' What they did not know was that the Cummins had not run out of power but a niggling air leak had forced the crew to stop the outfit in order to charge up the air tanks. Even though the Volvos were getting ever closer and there was no way they could stop, there was no panic for the Scammell. When the air tanks were full, the brakes were released and she went for the top from a standing start. Not only did she keep ahead of the Volvos but 'Betsy' left them behind and, as they eventually reached the summit, she was disappearing into the distance with the Cummins bellowing hard. Not so much a confrontation, more a 'no contest'.

Going down to Cockermouth, across to Maryport on the back road to Workington 'Betsy' disgraced herself. Again having to stop on a steep rise with low air pressure, the driver forgot to select neutral on the Self-Changing Gears eight-speed box. The consequence of revving the Cummins hard whilst in gear with the brakes locked on was to boil the oil in the semi-auto box. The fail-safe plug did its job by popping out but, as well as putting the vehicle temporarily out of commission, this caused the liquid contents of the gearbox to be spewed across the road. Even with massive amounts of sand spread liberally on top, the Volvos just could not cross this stretch of contaminated road. As the first one reached the sand the driving wheels span and the second Volvo just was not powerful enough to take the combination over. It took the help of a local AEC breakdown truck to tri-head the convoy before the bank was cleared for both the heavy loads and they could be laid up for the night. The second day found 'Betsy' with a new fail-safe plug and replenished with oil. As she entered the dock area of Workington she had the chance to redeem herself.

Two fierce hump-back bridges dominated the last stretch of road and Magnaload engineers had a hard job to ease the vehicles over them. With the use of sand and steel sheets, efforts were made to surmount the obstacles but the gradient still proved a terrific test to the hydraulic Scheuerle trailers. All the three fleet tractors were used with 'Betsy' being in an F89 sandwich. As they tried to cross the first bridge the leading F89 hit the steel plates and its driving wheels span. It was then up to 'Betsy' to push hard and force it over. She was the only tractor not to suffer from wheel-spin and as the second Volvo hit the bridging plates it, too, suffered from slipping. The Scammell, which had ended up pushing the first Volvo, now had to pull the second one, plus the 12 axles of Scheuerle and, of course, the 137 tons of crane. When 'Betsy' repeated this amazing feat with the second load, it was felt that she had more than made amends for her earlier indiscretion.

1980 saw the name Magnaload disappear as Peckstons, one of the joint owners, went out of business. However, most of the staff and equipment were unaffected for, with the forming of Mammoet-Econofreight, it was business as usual, although for 'Betsy' it meant yet another coat of paint this time in a more patriotic red, white and blue. A year later she was to have her finest hour when she was the main tractor in an operation to move the heaviest load ever to have travelled on roads in the UK. The SIF vessel weighed in at 476 tonnes but along with trailers, bolsters and other ancillary equipment the all-up weight was well over 700 tonnes. Frightening for you and me even to comprehend but for the old girl, supported by a Mammoet FTF, it was just a shrug of the shoulders and a bit more toe on the accelerator for driver John Angles. Well she had pulled a 1,000-ton module on site so anything less was well within her personal best. With performance like this it is obvious that Scammell are being modest when they rate the big Contractor for 240 tons gross operation.

Not only the ultra-heavyweights were hauled by the Contractor for quite a few of the lightweight versions were used in articulated form. 'Betsy', in fact, started life as an artic and was reputedly the largest low-loader west of Bristol. However, it was to be Wynns who were to get the best out of their lightweights with machines like JDW147F. One day it would be running about as an artic but the next day might have found it with a ballast box on its back and pulling one of the fleet's girder trailers.

The best example of the Contractor artic is undoubtedly Wynns' 'Renown', KAX395P. It had originally started life as a normal 240-ton 6 × 4 ballast tractor but, with the arrival of Sam Anderson's brainchild, the six-axle Nicolas semi-trailer, the Scammell found itself destined to be a horse of a different kind with a permanent bend in the middle. Different tyres were fitted and the rear-axle gear ratios were lifted slightly to give a better turn of speed, although working up to 150 tons gross as an artic was still well within its capacity. Five years later this special machine still has its admirers, not least of whom is a Lummus representative who greeted 'Renown' when she rolled back on to dry land in Scotland with a 105-ton regenerator from GEC Larne. Peter Wynn was accompanying the load and he was quick to sing the vehicle's praises as he said it was the only one of its kind, the best heavy-haulage artic in the land. Ten minutes later he wished he had kept his mouth shut for the Scammell could not get out of the docks. A greasy climbing road covered in morning dew afforded no grip to the tyres and it needed the help of a Leyland 6 × 6 breakdown truck before progress to Moss-morran could be continued.

This incident apart, 'Renown' performs very well but, like all Contractors, to get the best from them, you have to treat them right. Regular crew Alan and Tony Williams demonstrated this one day in their big Scammell, having with them a third man who was not really conversant with the quirks of the machine. Going up a long incline Alan shouted across to Tony, 'The wagon's not going too well today' and sure enough progress seemed to be getting slower and slower. Unknown to the third man all Alan was doing was simply easing slightly off the accelerator, but Tony's retort to this was, 'She certainly isn't, she must need a titbit'. 'Give her some sugar,' Tony shouted, so Alan leant out of the window and threw across a sugar lump which landed in a suitably placed dent right in the middle of the bonnet. As the sugar disappeared Alan put his foot down bringing a surge from the Scammell and a look of astonishment from the third man. Two more lumps were needed to clear the hill although, when the third man suggested this remedy to other drivers he was later to crew, their looks suggested he should perhaps be locked up somewhere secure.

Both Pickfords and Wynns thought the Contractor to be quite a tool. Numerous other operators had one or two of the big Scammells but not everybody thought they were ideal. To some they were too big, too numb, and in time of recession too expensive to buy and too impractical to keep in work all the time. What a lot of operators wanted was something just a bit smaller and yet still strong enough to pull the 100-ton load if and when required. Nothing in the Scammell range seemed to fit the bill for between the 6 × 4 Crusader, which was rated for 65 tons gtw, and the massive Contractor there seemed a yawning gap. People like Foden could offer to build a one-off special but it was the Europeans who were to step in and provide what the operators wanted.

Above One of four 270-ton generator transformers built by Parsons Peebles of Edinburgh is seen en route to the Longannet power station in Fife. These hauls were done between November 1968 and January 1971, being quite an early test for three of the new Contractors, SYO386F being the pusher at the rear. Between Granton and Rosyth on the Firth of Forth, the ro-ro ship *Kingsnorth Fisher* carried the 355 tons of load and trailer. **Below** Cummins pulls Rolls-Royce in this group move on December 7 1969. Brand-new, as yet unnamed, 'Challenger' heads the outfit and the 220-ton pressure vessel destined for ICI Wilton is seen crossing Victoria Bridge at Thornaby. The bridge had to be specially rechecked and upgraded before Head Wrightsons started on the manufacture of the vessel and so were assured that they would be able to get it out of the factory. The 12 rows of Crane Fruehauf bogies were those normally used on the girder trailer, which KVN860E is pushing hard from the rear.

Left John Robinson eases under the overhead structure of Newport Bridge, Middlesbrough, on his way to ICI Billingham in early 1970. The Contractor is in immaculately new condition and is still awaiting its 175 fleet number. The load is one of four UHDE vessels built by Whessoe, at its Ashmore works. The load's dimensions were 144 ft long, 16 ft diameter and 120 tons in weight, and it was carried on a pair of Crane 60-ton capacity bogies.

Left and below left December 19 1971 was a memorable day for Wynns, Scammell and the many by-standers who turned out to watch for, at the time, these were the largest loads hauled in the United Kingdom. Built in Holland, these petrochemical vessels weighed, in total, 511 tons and had to be road-hauled 17 miles to the Shell refinery at Stanlow.

Above 'Conqueror', lacking her name-plate but none of her strength, is seen in 1971 hauling Crane girder-trailer 789. Leading driver is Tommy Cranwell and he is seen threading his way through Birmingham with the first of four turbo generators destined for Didcot power-station.

Above right Jack Hill of Botley bought TRL924H from Mid Cornwall Contractors in 1972. His answer to the lack of room in the standard lightweight Contractor cab was to add on a further pod, originally used as the working compartment of a D8 Caterpillar.

Right TPY675H slips off this Hansa boat in Hull docks for a short haul to BP's Saltend refinery in about 1972. At 200 tons this Swedish reactor vessel was far too heavy for any pneumatic-tyred trailer in the Sunter fleet at the beginning of the 70s and thus the 'solids' were brought back into work.

Opposite page Ron Savage and 'Crusader' seen in June 1974 en route from Manchester to the Beetham paper-mill of Henry Cooke (1932) Ltd near Kendal. At 100 tons it wasn't exceptionally heavy but the geography of this part of the country meant that between Preston and Barrow-in-Furness, the load was carried on the back of a ro-ro ship.

This page and overleaf Of all the places on the map, distant Penzance is quite a memorable town to the Wynns crews, as these Richards Brothers photographs show. Getting this Ferranti transformer up to the Indians Queen substation near Newquay was hard enough for 'Challenger' and one of the lightweights but, as Roger Banfield will tell you, getting the empty outfit home can be just as difficult.

Above It took 900 of Wrekin Roadways bhp to ensure this stone-crusher got up into the ARC Edgehill quarry near Shrewsbury in about 1976. Not so much because of its 35-ton weight but, with gradients up to 1 in 6 on loose gravel, safety in numbers was preferred to heroic faith in the trusty Foden. **Below** At 81 tonnes, this kiln section is not the heaviest of loads hauled by Jimmy Goulding, but taking it from Hull to Hope in Derbyshire right through the centre of York was quite a test for Gino, Scammell and the eight-row Scheuerle trailer.

Left and below left Wynns expected a heavy work-load from their light-weight Contractors and not least of them was JDW147F, fleet number 185. She is shown coupled to a Scheuerle semi-trailer hauling an N class locomotive believed to be en route from Barry to Alresford in about 1973 and also with a ballast box, hauling one of the Crane girder-trailers.

Opposite page The Contractor could never be described as small but, whilst these 50-ft diameter silos are some of the largest loads 'Fear-nought' has ever moved, both load and towing vehicle were put into proper perspective by the size of Ris-don-Beasley's floating crane *Telford* as it loaded the silos on to the Nicolas trailer, which rolled on 256 tyres.

Left Robert Price of Beckenham recorded this Wynns transformer train approaching Mitchell on May 22 1977. The ducting used for the air-cushion equipment is clearly visible on the back of the Crane trailer but the hover principle probably wouldn't have been used on this haul for payload in the Parsons unit was only 125 tons.

This page In August 1978 Pickfords Heavy Haulage moved six loads which had been brought into Immingham docks aboard the Starman boats *Africa*, *America* and *Anglia*. The two heaviest were these 210- and 370-tonnes vessels measuring between 115 and 135 ft in length, which were to form part of an oil-residue upgrading processor being built by Lindsey Oil Refinery at South Killingholme.

Right One of the early, big load-outs performed by Pickfords was the movement of this Motherwell Bridge module in July 1977. At 1,050 tons, it was a weight which had to be slowly winched on board, PGO712E and SYO384F, the two 240-ton Contractors, simply acting as brakes on this occasion.

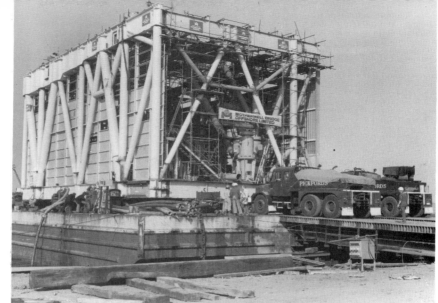

Right and overleaf Sunter–ITM moved over 50 prefabricated pipe-racks and modules up at the Shetlands Sullom Voe site. At 60 ft high and up to 450 tonnes in weight, working all hours of the clock, they regularly caught the photographer's eye. All of Sunters' big tractors spent time at the terminal although their mainstay was HVN397N, the Contractor which went to the Persian Gulf for some time at the beginning of the eighties.

Right Sunters HVN397N alongside Wynns 'Challenger' are seen in the premises of Mother-well Bridge at Leith waiting to ease back towards the barge with this second 700-ton module. The shot, taken in about 1977, shows the first big load-out of the newly formed Sunter-ITM combine.

Below The complexity of ICI Wilton does not lend itself to building new installations right inside the works. The answer to the problem is building in module form, then moving this by road into the required position. Peter Clemmett and 'Fearnought' coupled to Nicolas axles are ample strength for a move of less than a mile.

Above December 1979 saw 'Betsy' on her head-to-head confrontation with the F89s travelling between Carlisle and Cockermouth, her destination being Workington. The load was one of two 137-ton railway cranes built by Cowans Sheldon and destined for New Zealand.

Left This 200-ton crane was needed for ship-repair work at Kingston Yard, Glasgow, and was eventually moved no more than 500 yds. Three suggestions for moving the crane were made to its owners, two of which would have taken four months and one month respectively. Pickfords did the job in two days although I doubt if Crane Fruehauf ever thought their girder-trailer would carry anything as spectacular as this.

Wynns Heavy Haulage Contractors rarely overtake anything but here 'Talisman' eases past the watching Spencer David, hauling 180 ton of rotor — just over half the weight supported on the massive Nicolas girders to the right of the picture.

Wrekin Roadways' 20-row Nicolas girder-trailer is seen on its first haul as it pauses for breath at the specially constructed abnormal-load bridge built on box crossroads of the A34 and A500. The 258-ton load was destined for the Littlebrook power-station.

Roger Banfield sprints to catch up 'Talisman' as she hauls one of the Littlebrook boilers manufactured by NEI John Thompson of Wolverhampton. 17 rows of Nicolas running gear were needed to support the 105 ft long load, the all-up combination weight being near to 400 tonnes.

Constable Derek Barker stands guard as Gino tries to get round this awkward sign post near the Marton Country Club on Teesside. Pulling one of three similar loads made by Foster Wheelers of Hartlepool, YVN308T made the circuitous trip round to Teesport on Sunday July 29 1979 in less than six hours of sunshine.

'Betsy's' finest hour was when she was the stalwart tractor in the movement of this impressive 476 tonnes, 193 ft 9 ins long SIF vessel into Esso's Fawley refinery in July 1981.

UVN44S is seen heading for Mossmorran in July 1982 with this 91 ft long, 21 ft wide vessel, with all-up weight being about 180 tons. The two following Volvos are running with 120 tyres on their Nicolas trailers with loads of 96 and 106 tonnes in weight.

She may be an old ICI rebuild but UVN44S can still pull her weight as she showed in April 1983 with the site haul of this 384 tons, 240 ft long flotation tank which was to form the side of an oil rig being constructed at Ardissie, Scotland.

This was one of three modules, moved by Mammoet Econofreight in May 1983, destined for Conoco's Hutton field. At 875 tons in weight it was rather heavy even for 'Betsy', who is now rather mature in years and she was simply acting as a compressor to put air into the trailers braking system as winches pulled it forward.

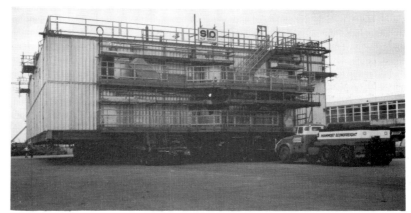

Jimmy Goulding, in the rebuilt Sunters' Scammell, heads up Albert Lowes whilst Peter Clemmett in 'Fearnought' pulls Malcolm Johnson, as this 1200 tons of Whessoe module makes its way on to a site at Heysham, Lancashire, during the summer of 1983.

Above and above right *Renown*, perhaps the biggest artic in the land, is quite a workhorse for the Wynn's fleet. She is seen coupled to a nine-axle semi-trailer turning onto the A92 near Inverkeithing with a 105-ton regenerator for Mossmorran. She is also pictured coupled to her original six-axle Nicolas going up the access pier at Fleetwood with an 85-tonne engine for Northern Ireland.

Below What a line up! 3,147 tonnes or thereabouts, including the drapes, was the weight of this module being pushed backwards towards the River Tees in late August 1983. Cleveland Bridge's site at Port Clarence was the location of this mountain move although Sunters' drivers rarely get excited about things like this now. They find it more interesting to pull 300 tons over the likes of Beattock, Shap or Stanedge for, after your first big site move, every other one is just the same. For those interested in tyres there were 1,088 of them taking the strain.

9. The European alternative

With legislation in Sweden allowing certain general-haulage vehicles to operate at weights nearly twice those permitted in the UK, it was not surprising that when the Volvo F88 came to these shores it soon built up a reputation for strength, durability and driver acceptance, although it was to be certain of the heavier F89s which were to find their way into the select 100-ton club. Magnaload brought two of these 6 × 4s into operation in 1976 and not only were they pleased with a 180-ton gtw rating at 7½ per cent gradability for an 'off the peg' machine, but they were also particularly pleased with a delivery time, including passage from Sweden, of less than four weeks. Heart of the '89s was Volvo's own six-cylinder TDA 120 engine which produced close to 300 bhp from a very small engine by means of optimum use of a turbocharger. Driving through a very low-geared back bogie meant that the vehicle's top speed was not quite 40 mph, although the gearbox did have 16 different ratios. To those not in the know there are really only four different gear positions for the driver to select. Once he has changed up to fourth gear, operation of an electrical switch changes the 'range' to a higher band so that fifth gear is back in the same position as first and so on up to eighth gear. All of these eight gears can be split into half steps by another electrical switch called a 'splitter', thus doubling up the number of ratios to 16. Still difficult to understand? Well, ask Sunters' driver Tony Swan if it's hard to follow, for he was trained to get the best performance out of the high-revving Foden two-stroke which had 12 gears using two different gear levers. He now blames the ever-increasing size of his stomach on the relative ease of driving his current 16-speed Volvo.

To suit Magnaload's specifications the two Volvo F89s were equipped with inboard winching facilities, although at Manchester it was their road strength which was really put to the test. Anyone having an intimate knowledge of the NDSM petrochemical vessels moved from Pomona dock to the Carrington refinery will know that the job was not without its problems. The original plan was for the vessels to be moved by means of end suspension, ie, supported at either end by 'book ends', so that the running height would allow them to creep under the motorway flyovers. But when it was discovered that the supporting structures were not strong enough, the loads had to be carried straight on top of the Scheuerle bogies which meant that even with adjustable suspension they could not get under anything. Well, if you can't go under, you just have to go over, but it was only done with the closest of co-operation from Greater Manchester police who closed the motorway to other motorists for 20 minutes early one Sunday morning to allow the loads to travel down the wrong carriageway. One thing that could not be faulted was the strength of the Volvos for, even with each outfit having an all-up weight approaching 250 tons, Maurice Race still recalls four upward gear changes as the two loads in convoy reached a steady 25 mph down the traffic-free motorway. These Volvos had made their mark but it was over the following seven years that they proved they were not just a nine-day wonder and, at the time of writing, they are still going strong. No matter how good a product you make, it still needs to be handled with appropriate driver sympathy and that probably more than anything else is why even now clutch failure is still a very rare occurence. Drivers were rewarded even further when Volvo updated their range with the well-liked F12 models. Mike Cave's Planthaul company of Bedford were to operate three of these 180-ton rated machines across the length and breadth of Europe, although his operating preference found them generally always in articulated form. He was, however, to adopt a strange technique, widely used on the continent, whereby when power was required his multi-axled heavy haulage artics were helped along by a ballasted tractor pusher.

Volvo were not the only Swedish company to

make massive inroads into the UK heavy haulage scene as Scania, too, were to get a big following especially because of the high standard of driver comfort they offered. Coming into the UK in the early 1980s was the R142E 6 × 4 range which were to be rated for 150 tons gtw operation whilst even the small four-wheelers could run up to 80 tons gtw when being operated at the slower speeds required in 'special types' operation. However, it was the earlier left-hand drive 146 range which first established a Scania presence amongst the select 100-tonners. James Watkinson Ltd, of Keighley, had already thoroughly tried the Scania range so, when an even stronger tractor was wanted, a bonneted 6 × 4, registration number BDB369T, came to West Yorkshire. Do not let that drawl of Keith Watkinson's fool you for, even though the 146 was Scania's best, Keith was bright enough to know that for what he was going to ask from it, a few more inches had to be specified on top of the standard tractor wheelbase. With no worries about overall length a full sleeper cab was the first addition to be added by Unity Conversions of Bolton. With a smart paint job to finish things off 'Ymir' took to the road. Was this Yorkshire's most impressive rig? Certainly, but Howard Nunnick will tell you that 'Ymir' was, of course, a giant in Norse mythology.

The regular driver was Les Hutchinson who was extremely impressed by the way in which the vehicle performed. Its engine was the relatively standard lightly turbocharged DS1401 Scania V8 which produced 375 bhp at 2,000 rpm from its 14.2 litres. The transmission took the power via the twin-plate clutch to the ten-speed gearbox (five selections in a high and low range) then to the hub-reduction double-drive bogie. A lot was expected from the vehicle for as the ex-Sparrows Scammell Contractor left for Sri Lanka, the mantle of fleet flagship fell firmly on to 'Ymir's' shoulders. Running either as a ballasted tractor or in articulated form with Comet-to trailer beds and running gear, Watkinsons worked the vehicle hard. Moving a 164 ft long crane section from AB Cranes at Telford to South Killingholme in Lincolnshire created a lot of controversy. There was no trouble for the Scania on the 250-mile, six-day cross-country haul, but many arguments centred on whether this section, or one hauled earlier which went to Norway, was the longest load moved on roads in the UK over a substantial distance. Record keepers are well aware that the 193 ft 6 ins SIF vessel moved by Mammoet-Econofreight, over a 5-mile haul at Fawley, betters this by some distance. There was not a lot of weight on the crane section job but when a massive Manitowg site crane was moved in one piece at Tillicoultry near Stirling, the scales would have shown that

the combination weight had topped the 200-ton mark.

The transmission took quite a hammering with work like this and the five gears in the low range of the box did what amounted to a lifetime's work every six months. As the prospect of moving even heavier loads loomed, Keith Watkinson knew it was now time to utilise those extra inches he had specified in the vehicle's wheelbase. So during the 1982 Christmas/New Year break, Tony Bairstow, the fleet's head engineer, took out the Scania ten-speed box and replaced it with a nine-speed Fuller which drove through a two-speed Spicer transfer box. There were now 18 gears to play with and, with crawler first having a ratio of 27.8:1, precisionist Mr Bairstow knew that with the vehicle let loose in bottom gear and the engine running at 1,000 rpm, it would take 3 mins 46 secs for it to cross the small company yard. The spread of ratios also meant that the Scania's new top speed was a rapid 55 mph, ideal for homeward-bound empty motorway running.

In 1983 Michael Albone became 'Ymir's' regular driver and, with the addition of a little more ballast when running in locomotive form, he found the modified Scania to be better balanced and even more impressive. Even more was expected of it as the loads got heavier and heavier. At 120 tons the concrete beams hauled out to the new M65 were particularly testing. The severe climb away from their manufacturers, Faircloughs of Accrington, certainly made Mick appreciate the extra spread of low ratios. Two even longer loads of concrete running at 170 tons gross were hauled without incident from Dow Mac, Tallington, near Grantham to Middlesbrough but in Scotland the Scania was forced to admit defeat.

The present-day heavy haulier finds himself asked to move weights which less than ten years ago no one would have dreamed were feasible. True, these moves are on site not roads and of course the distance may be measured in yards not miles, but four figures worth of weight in the load is still heavy even though it may now be routine. 'Ymir' was working at UEI on Clydebank with tractors of Sarens and Johnstones. When a tractor is pulling together with other units, the most important man on the job is the banksman. He is the man who coordinates the moving of the load and his stop or go signals must be strictly obeyed. There are, of course, times when one of the tractors may get wheelspin through insufficient ballasting, or it might just stall through too high a gear being engaged. Whatever the reason the result is that if one tractor is trying to do the job of two or three all on its own then, unless it is a member of the super club, something normally has to give. What gave with 'Ymir' was its propshaft which went with a mighty bang as it tried to pull 1,000 tons unassisted. Even though such a pull seemed to be asking far too much from the Scania, its pride was slightly dented. One certain way to prevent this type of catastrophe to your transmission is to utilise an automatic gearbox, an exercise conducted by yet another European.

The Swedes had nearly seven years' start on Van Doorne Automobielfabriecken (DAF) for they did not bring their first units into the UK until 1973. Their pedigree was just as solid and, although their standard heavy haulage 6 × 4 tractors were until quite recently only rated at 110 tons train weight, they have had a member in the select club for some time.

Outwardly WJH288T looks like thousands of other 2800s but clamber in or around it, or better still listen to it drive off rapidly, and you will realise that appearances are deceptive and this DAF is very special indeed. The machine culminated from discussions between Tom Llewellyn of Econofreight Transport and Robert Kieft of DAF. Both parties were interested in the development of a heavier-than-normal, automatic-transmission heavy-haulage tractor, although the experiment did have its financial constraints. Tom quite fancied the ZF Transmatic version but with DAF having already conducted extensive field work with the Allison HT700 series, it was the latter which found its way into the FTT2805 DKS360 chassis. There were to be only five forward gears but all the driver had to do was to engage the two-five notch, which meant that the Allison then selected gears automatically. The machine was obviously a prototype and no matter how much theorising was done on the drawing boards and test bench, it was to be road work which was to sort the vehicle out.

Steve Ford, like most of the DAF's other drivers, found the vehicle excellent to drive, although at times he was concerned about the loss of power from the standard 2800 engine which was naturally absorbed through using an automatic gearbox. Going eastwards on the old A66 with an RB crawler machine the climb out of Appleby town proved just too much for the DAF. Bottom gear was engaged but there was not enough power to propel the vehicle and its 70-ton load forwards.

Taking a 27 ft wide fabrication through the 28 ft wide Tyne Tunnel was another tough test for the DAF and it is natural to think that an automatic vehicle would be ideal for this slow meticulous move. When the tunnel pointed upwards it did in fact prove its point but on the initial descent driver Ford had his work cut out. Even in first gear the automatic box allowed the vehicle to run up to ten mph, which was far too fast for this part of the move. The hydraulic retarder created too much heat rise so the service brakes had to be dabbed continually as the outfit ran deep below the River Tyne.

Both these problems were solved by lowering the back axle ratios making the vehicle far better for heavier work. It naturally enforced a reduction in the machine's top speed but the automatic DAF is now found to be a boon in the assorted Econofreight fleet. Unlike most heavy-haulage tractors the vehicle is adaptable enough to run in general haulage pulling any of their assorted short, long or low multi-axle semi-trailers. But as the heavier work has increased nationwide for the Teeside operator, the DAF is more often to be found with 20 tons of ballast on its back ready to head up the rest of the fleet's heavy-haulage tractors. Only rarely do they need a hand when the roads are flat but when they are going up mountain sides, the most testing of terrain to a heavy-haulage man, then the DAF gets called in to perform. Its Allison automatic box means that the machine is always in the right gear, the slick changes ruling out that awful 'snatch' which can occur when two vehicles with manual gearboxes attempt to change gear in concert. It can still be relied on to pull its weight independently, as the site operations manager, Eric Pinchin, was pleased to find when he was stuck with the problem of moving a massive Air Products cold-box on site at Mossmorran. The fleet's Scammell S24 was temporarily out of commission undergoing bodywork repairs whilst the hard-working Volvo N10 was also resting with a wheel problem, so there was nothing else for it but to try WJH. The 238 tons of box was supported by 13 rows of Nicolas running gear, so that the combination weight would obviously be in excess of the 300-ton mark, but the DAF did not bat an eyelid and moved it about with no trouble. She may not be one of the club's superstars but WJH288T has more than proved her claim to membership.

One could question the necessity of producing as odd a vehicle as WJH for, surely, there is more than enough choice on the market to satisfy demand? DAF for one would not support this theory for it is on mobile test-beds like this that a lot of practical information is gained. The arduous work which their bonneted tippers did in Luxembourg, Nigeria and Zimbabwe has now given them the ability to rate the drive axles on their new tractors at 20 tons each, ie, 40 tons on the back bogie — capacity which only the big Contractor used to be able to offer. It is true that the automatic gearing is not now a part of the transmission, although this type of

propulsion is an integral part of possibly the most powerful tractor covered in this book. Its prowess has been established through on-site, back-to-back tugs of war with other tractors (a pastime indulged in by bored heavy-haulage drivers). The on-lookers sometimes have difficulty guessing what make this odd vehicle may be — Bedford is the most common guess.

Having customers throughout the world eager to buy their modular trailers, the French company of Nicolas had quite a problem when the recipients also wanted to buy something to pull the hydraulic load carriers as part of a complete heavy haulage package. Their fellow countrymen at Berliet produced some specials but this source dried up when the Renault influence made them concentrate on more routine types of machine. Nicolas even tried to interest Scammell in a form of joint venture but this never really took off so the French then decided that, if they used the best of components available, then surely they could assemble their own prime movers. The result of this assembling is the Tractomas range which covers anything from a 6 x 4 unit right up to an 8 x 8. The choice of engine varies from the V12 Mercedes or six-cylinder Cummins to the two-stroke Detroit, with the most powerful option in the 8 x 8 being the V16 GM producing 800 bhp at 2,100 rpm.

Sunters were not really interested in an eight-wheeler but when their TR66C4C 6 x 6 came to Northallerton its Cummins KTA 450 power pack made it one of the most powerful vehicles of the fleet. Peter Sunter had been very pleased with the performance of his Titans but he still felt these were a shade on the light side for the increasing amount of heavy module work which his company was attracting. The Tractomas seemed to have more beef about it and, as Sunters were able to offer Nicolas a toe-hold in the UK heavy haulage scene, it meant that both parties were able to strike up a very good business deal.

Chauffeur number one was Albert Lowes and, although he had 20 years' experience driving anything from Rotinoffs to Contractors, he still had to go back to the books to learn how to drive the Nicolas. The big difference in the transmission is the eight forward, four reverse Clark 'powershift' gearbox which is coupled to a CL8612 torque converter. As on the semi-automatic box used on

the Scammell, the clutch pedal is dispensed with but, in the case of the Nicolas, the driver has a lot more to think about than just pushing or pulling on a stubby lever. The gearbox is like an elongated letter E and setting away from rest when unladen the lever can be simply put in the torque eighth position and the automatic box will eventually sort everything out by itself, although when laden it's rather different. To ensure maximum control of the machine, the first selection of the driver is torque first. The converter will then ensure a smooth take-off but once the engine rpm dial coincides with the torque converter rpm dial then the driver can slide the gearlever sideways locking in to first gear. As speed is built up and an upward change desired, the operating lever is shifted across and up from the locked first to the torque second position. When the two rpm dials coincide again, the lever is slid over, second gear is locked and gears changed up in a similar fashion until the desired road speed is reached.

You also have to read the books to understand which is the lowest gear as the crew of the similar machine belonging to Brackmills found as they were en route to Workington with a heavy load. They were locked into first gear but found that in no way would the Nicolas surmount the Cumbrian incline. Actually they should have been in the torque first position and then the converter would have worked everything out for there is no weight, as yet, which the Nicolas has failed to pull.

Heavy site movements form a large part of the current Sunter work-load with anything up to four of their largest fleet tractors employed on any one job. The Nicolas is now tractor No 1 and although when working in combination with other units drivers are bound to argue who was pulling the most weight, at Heysham the facts speak for themselves. On one occasion the load was a massive Whessoe module, its destination the new power-station, the all-up weight 1,387 tons and when it had to be moved away from the barge at a moment's notice it was the Nicolas which did the job. The back end dropped and dug in as the cab lifted when Albert, the driver, attempted to move it but, as the Soma axles squirmed for grip on their Michelin tyres, it was only the inertia which was broken as the mass moved on. The gradient was close to 1 in 30 yet still the Tractomas-Lowes combination kept going and, were it not for the abandoned Contractors parked in the way, then Albert would surely have made the top unassisted. Nicolas may describe the vehicle in their brochure as fit for occasional use at 250 tons gtw, although Sunters have found that at five times the figure it can still do the job.

The only problem is one which affects all vehicles equipped with automatic gearboxes and that, of course, is the dissipation of transmission heat. Massive cooling fans are thermostatically controlled but even these were found to be lacking on one occasion when fourth gear malfunctioned forcing a gearbox rebuild. This was put down to an excessive internal temperature and to counter any such recurrence a manual override was fitted so that the fans could be started as the vehicle began to work hard. Albert has found that, for some reason, it is when he is running empty that he has to keep the closest watch on the oil-temperature guage. 'Empty', of course, is 48 tons of ballasted tractor hauling 52 tons of unladen Nicolas axles which makes 100 tons

capable of 45-50 mph with little difficulty.

With a predominance of site moves on the Nicolas itinerary, long-distance road hauls are few and far between but taking a 120-ton kiln section from Head Wrightsons at Thornaby to Avonmouth gave the Tractomas a chance to stretch its legs. Routed via the M62, M6 and M5 the Cummins was able to show how much power it could produce and even with a strict police escort the load arrived three days early. So if you want to move 1,200 tons of module 300 yards or 120 tons of kiln section 300 miles, then the Tractomas can certainly do it for you unless you would like to try something different. . .

Quite a handful for driver Ernie Pickersgill was this Head Wrightson dock gate hauled from Thornaby to Middlesbrough in August 1981. Bound for Seaham Harbour it was 70 tons in weight and 31 ft wide.

Magnaload's two Volvos are seen en route from Pomona dock to the Carrington refinery at Manchester. Plans of this move had to be altered at the eleventh hour, but one thing which couldn't be faulted was the strength of the F89s which were running at close to 250 tons all-up weight.

The ex-Magnaload Volvos have certainly shown they aren't a nine-day wonder and at seven years of age are still working for their keep. RAJ530R is seen heading up this convoy en route to Mossmorran in July 1982 with a 134-ton load on its ten-axle trailer.

HVN396N was Sunters' first big F89 and driver Malcolm Johnson is seen in the ICI Wilton complex in 1979 hauling this lengthy module on two Crane bogies. Along with 397N, this F89 went to the Persian Gulf for some time in 1980 as part of Hercules International Transport.

Scammells are strong but even they need a hand on occasion, as two of Sunters' F89s helping to move this Motherwell Bridge module show. With the ever increasing size of site loads, the modern-day photographer like John Cameron of Edinburgh has a lot of climbing to do to capture the best type of shot on offer.

Above HEE313N is TSL's faithful F89 and is seen in 1977 en route from Dunkinfield to Liverpool docks hauling ten rows of Goldhoffer axles. The 120-ton vessel was then shipped to the Shetlands Sullom Voe oil terminal.

Left Geoff Johnson of Barton uprated this Scania 141 to just below 150 tons gross although it still ranked itself as a member of the select club. It took this 154 ft long Davy vessel from Manchester to Liverpool docks in 1981 but at 18 ft high its route was a headache as it included all parts of Lancashire and Southport sea front.

Right and below right Watkinson's Scania 146 can either operate as an artic or in ballasted tractor form, the company making varied use of their Cometto axles and beds. Automatic steering of the rear three axles make this lengthy outfit less of a handful as 'Ymir' inches this Greens of Wakefield steam boiler into position.

Right Econofreight had two of these 26 ft 9 ins wide fabrications to move through the Tyne Tunnel which was only 28 ft at its widest. Following their automatic DAF was Watkinson's Scania 146 and this shot by Tom Llewellyn taken at 2:00 am shows how tight a job it really was.

'Ymir' is seen leaving AB Cranes at Telford with this 164 ft long crane section. Six days were needed for the 250-mile cross-country journey to South Killingholme in Lincolnshire.

With the scales tipped at over 200-tons combination weight when Watkinsons moved this site crane at Tillicoultry near Stirling, their Scania needed a helping hand from the unballasted DAF to ease it round a tight corner near its destination.

'Ymir' seen on April 20 1982 in the premises of Head Wrightsons on Teesside with an internal move, where the combination weight was close to 240 tonnes.

Right Projector Transport Services of Newport Pagnell managed the movement of four buoyancy tanks, made by Elgin Engineering, destined for Ardeseir where the rig for British Hydracarbons Morecombe Bay field was under construction. Glazepen's new Scania 142 is seen going through Forres, summer 1983, with one of the 50-ton vessels which were 9 ft 3 ins in diameter and 120 ft 6 ins long.

Below right Glazepen's Scania is seen having to adopt different steering techniques with one of five similar loads that were road-hauled from Bury St Edmunds to Felixstowe, eventually destined for Teesside in early 1983. Not a great deal of weight but at 130 ft long they were quite a handful.

Below Steve Ford has just left Morris Cranes of Loughborough with one of two 49-ton, 114 ft long girders that were hauled across to Liverpool docks. The automatic DAF is hauling Dyson low-line bogies. The petrol price really seems to date the photograph!

Opposite page Coupled to a Nicolas semi-trailer, the DAF is discharging this boat into the Wear at Sunderland in 1980. Built by two men at Easington Lane, the vessel is used as a supply boat at one of the North Sea oil rigs.
This page The automatic DAF now finds itself regularly called on to double head other fleet tractors if their situation calls for a helping hand. The cylinder vessel is one of the numerous loads hauled to Mossmorran, whilst the box-type load is being helped up the steep gradient into Heighington village, June 1982. The latter was one of 39 loads destined for Balipakpan, Indonesia, being 20 ft high, 20 ft wide and weighing 134 tons.

Left and below left Site work is the main part of the Tractomas itinerary but it occasionally shows its paces with lighter, road work. The 177-ton Head Wrightson vessel was one of four moved in convoy to Hartlepool docks for export to Russia in 1982 whilst the Foster Wheeler 125-ton boiler was hauled to the same docks in July 1983.

Opposite page Heanor Haulage and Geoff Johnson were two of the many operators who put to work the DAF 2800 and 3300 tractors. With a rating of 150 tons gross train weight they only just merited inclusion in the select 100-ton club, but the hauliers were more impressed with a 40-ton rear-bogie capacity which gave great peace of mind when operating the tractors in articulated guise.

Left How do you move something like this? Mammoet-Econofreight say you have to move it carefully. The Anglo-Swedish quartet have just winched what are described as two-in-one rough decks BDO 2 and BDO 3 at RGC Methil in September 1983. It was then halved and loaded out onto a waiting barge even more carefully. The weight of this giant-size dinner table was 1,750 tons.

10. Something different

For eight years now the leader of non-conformity has produced his specials from the corner of a garage sitting on the site of the old New Langley colliery. Laceyfields Road, 'Mecca' for many heavy-haulage enthusiasts, is similar to any other minor housing-estate road but, unlike the others, the residents are well used to the early morning bark of the strident Detroit diesel. No one can complain because, long before the houses were built, Heanor Haulage had centred their diverse operations on this sleepy part of Derbyshire. Peter Searson heads the company and he is an inspiration to others to do things in the way which they think they should be done.

Contrary to common belief, Peter is a great admirer of the Scammell product, although his request for a version to suit his needs fell on deaf ears. All he wanted was the high-powered Detroit engine coupled to a multi-speed manual Fuller transmission in his Contractors but, alas, Scammell were not to answer his calls. His way out of this difficulty is well known in the heavy-haulage world for out of that garage came ONN686P, HHT number 001. The chassis had started life as PNU772K, a relatively straightforward lightweight Contractor although by the time Mr Searson and his men had finished with it, it was only barely recognisable. A Volvo F88 cab sat behind the Detroit engine and the vehicle had eight wheels resting on the ground. Even the wheel configuration was different as six out of the eight were on the back bogie. True, the leading one of the three axles was not driving but it did mean the tractor could support loadings which were never dreamed of if you wished to operate conventional articulated outfits.

HHT 002 soon came off 'the production line' but unlike its predecessor it had been half-way round the world and back before it landed in Derbyshire. Manufactured originally for a customer in the Middle East, it was rejected by the authorities out there for political reasons. The left-hand drive,

Cummins-engined Contractor found its way back to the UK and ended up even more strangely in the shipbuilding yard of John Browns at Glasgow. Unused and unwanted it lay there till Mr Searson picked it up, brought it back to Heanor and put it to work, registered as XRA297L, still in its conventional Scammell form. When subsequently changed into an HHT, it appeared with a new registration, SAL513R, a Detroit engine and Volvo cab but, unlike 001, it was of more conventional 6 × 4 shape yet it did have 52 different gears for the driver to play with. For those who may have palpitations at the prospect of trying to remember where all the gears are, it should be explained that there are only five main positions for the gear lever. Four positions in the main Fuller gearbox have a high and low range which doubles the gears to eight but when in high range these four gears can be halved with a splitter making a total of 12. An extra low, crawler gear brings the total to 13 but these are multiplied to 52 when they have passed through a four-speed Spicer auxiliary gearbox. To reassure those without scientific qualifications, 'Sal's' regular drivers only normally use the top 39 ratios. HHT 003 bore the registration BAL600T and its new gleaming red and white exterior belied the fact that is had already spent one hard lifetime of work in the ICI Tunstead quarry at Buxton as an articulated dumper in its Contractor form.

The three HHTs were the backbone of the heavy side of Heanor Haulage but, as the recession gripped in the early '80s, things were about to change. Peter really wanted to build 004 to a slightly different specification but, as there was only work for two of the big tractors, it meant 003 was sold to Shepherd Hill of Chesterfield and 002 went to GCS Johnson of Barton. In theory 'Sal' should have been past her best but the HHT injected a new strength into the middleweight Scania fleet. Bob Cook was the vehicle's regular driver and coming from a 141 it was to be quite a change. Only one instruction followed the vehicle north from Derbyshire and that was, 'Never put the HHT into first gear and put your foot down, for if you do the power from the engine will just tear the vehicle in half'.

Taking a 71 RB machine on to site at Healeyside, Northumberland, really tested men and machine. Grossing about 100 tons with the Nicolas semi-trailer it was not that heavy but inclines of 1 in 6 and steeper ensured that everyone had to work hard. The customer had laid on an old 6 × 6 Constructor to help passage and with that on the front the steepest part of the haul was surmounted. The HHT virtually pushed the Scammell up the hill, although a wagon coming the other way had to shoot off rather briskly into the nearside ditch to avoid colliding with the crawling load. He was extricated by tying a line from his rear on to the back of the low-loader and Bob pulled him out as he eased forward, thus showing that another 10 tons or so made little difference to the Detroit. With 3 miles to the site Bob found himself confronted with another 1 in 6 climb but this time accompanied by vicious bends. As there was no Scammell available for double heading there was no choice but to select 14th gear and go for the top solo. The Detroit did not falter but, as the hill got steeper, the weight was transferred backwards so, no matter how much the steering wheel was turned, 'Sal' just kept going straight on and would not take the bend. Bob was forced to dip the clutch but, even though he banged the brakes on, the outfit began sliding backwards on the greasy road surface. Quick thinking by trailerman David Lupton prevented a calamity for he quickly dropped the hydraulic suspension on the trailer throwing the bed straight on to the road and preventing any further rearward progress.

Bob may have recalled his uncle Siddle Cook's old Foden faced with a similar dilemma when it was moving excavators near Frosterly in Durham's Weardale 20 years earlier. It, too, reared off the ground when it encountered this type of corner and its crew had to chain a farm tractor on to the front of the Foden and literally pull it sideways round the corner. There was no such improvisation needed on this occasion for, with the old Scammell brought back on to the scene, its addition to the front gave directional stability to 'Sal' and she made it to the site without further incident.

'Sal' had proved what she could do but she was also to prove what weight she could pull when she became closely involved with Sarens of Belgium in heavy North Sea oil-module movements. In the Scottish yards she was working in combination with other units but at the deep water berth in Hartlepool she moved over 400 tons completely unassisted. Even this great weight did not warrant selection of

first gear and Bob just moved her off in fifth.

This demonstrates the prowess of the HHT, but the Heanor men reckon it is 004 which is the best of the bunch. Powered by the mighty Caterpillar type 3406 engine, 370 bhp is developed, which is slightly less than the previously favoured Detroit, although the better spread of torque brings nothing but praise from the regular driver, Peter Elgie. Transmission is by the 15-speed Fuller driving through a four-speed Spicer. Bearing the registration of XRA790Y, the chassis, similar to 003, originally started life as an ICI dumper, but the Searson formula now allows this mountain mover easily to top the maximum speed permitted on UK motorways. A company spokesman said there are definitely no plans to build another HHT, yet if you look hard enough through the collection of bits and pieces accumulated by Mr Searson, you will find yet another old Contractor dumper chassis. It may be covered in a thick layer of dust but, for those who want to see it, the figures 005 can easily be seen.

To the vast majority of us a visit to the annual motor show is a big social event. A chance to look at some very exotic sports cars and to see trucks especially smartened up for the week. All in all a break from work and a brief glance at Utopia, but when Chris Miller pushed open the doors of Kelvin Hall in 1977, the motor show was his idea of a supermarket. He was only shopping for one vehicle but he had a list in his pocket of requirements which had to be met. A new contract was in the offing and so testing was it to be that Chris felt he should itemise what he wanted from his machine before he spoke to the manufacturers. It had to be capable of pulling an all-up combination weight of 210 tons and climbing a 1 in 10 gradient whilst rolling, but it also had to be able to produce a 50 mph top speed when running empty. Its vital statistics should be no more than 8 ft 2½ ins wide, 22 ft in overall length and it should have a turning circle of no more than 55 ft. This ideal vehicle would be fitted with a sleeper cab, be able to operate either as an artic or as a ballasted tractor and be fitted with a torque converter. Anything else? Well, the price had to be right and, of course, he wanted a reasonable delivery date. Chris was ready to concede on some of his points, although the vehicle he eventually bought satisfied nearly all the criteria.

Scammell were the first firm he consulted but, with the S26 range still not on the drawing board, the Contractor was found to be rather long and could not meet the demanding small turning circle requirement. Both Foden and Volvo reassured Chris they could produce a special vehicle for the job, but the simple and sturdy machines which were to catch his eye were on the Mack stand. This

Having hauled in excess of 80 locomotives of all shapes and sizes; Mike Lawrence of Burnham on Sea has built up a reputation of expertise in this field of heavy haulage. His current fleet flagship is this Interstater UYC39W, which is rated for 145 tons gross operation. The Mack is pictured in 1982 hauling 34007 from the Barry graveyard across to Plymouth, combination weight being about 100 tons. The Transquip trailer has a self-steering rear axle and Lawrence's modifications allow 40 ft of railway line on its deck.

period of the 1970s had seen a great deal of pressure by the American truck makers to get into the UK market. The chance offered by Millers to jump into this area of heavy haulage was very attractive to Mack so, when the list was produced, it was not discounted as being totally unreasonable but seen as a target to aim for. Chris was very impressed by the time and effort put in by both the UK and American high-ranking personnel but the thing which must have swayed Millers into clinching the deal was just the sheer charisma created by the Bulldog. The Preston company was a small one by the standards of the heavy-haulage business but when they bought a vehicle which was so totally different people just had to sit up and take notice of them. Regular driver Peter Beasley will tell you that five years later that aura still exists for everywhere

he goes the Mack just magnetises the onlookers ensuring he gets very little peace and quiet.

Built in America the Interstater was powered by the famous cooled turbocharged Maxidyne engine. It produced just in excess of 300 bhp but, at 1,150 ft/lb, it gave 25 per cent more torque than any other other engine then in general use. There were 12 forward selections in the gearbox but one item the Americans would not fit was a torque converter. At Millers insistence, however, they did arrange for Mack UK to fit one before delivery. The result of the vehicle's specification was virtually as Chris had demanded. The only slightly different thing about the mechanical side of the Mack was that the winch was driven from an independent four-cylinder Ford engine and not by a more normal power take-off facility.

Named after what was then the strongest dog in the world, 'Bonzo Bear' took to the road and was immediately put to the test moving the Markham taps — at 150 tons the heaviest load Millers have shifted. The all-up weight was well over the 200-ton mark with their destination being the revolutionary Dinorwic power station.

From Chesterfield to Manchester over the Pennines is a harsh enough haul, but that was followed by the pull from Port Penryhn to the site. Even when it reached its destination the Mack was expected to inch its loads into some extraordinary positions inside the mountain, a task which would have severely tested any tractor. 'Bonzo Bear' did, in fact, hiccup in its early weeks but the back-up service given by its manufacturers meant that none of the loads was late in delivery. Modifications were made to the rear bogie by Mack but, after observations made by driver Beasley that the tractor performed far better when the torque converter was not there, Chris Miller had to admit he was wrong in overruling Mack's original insistence that it was not really compatible with their specification. The magic box was removed from the transmission and since those early days the tractor has performed without incident. This still seems hard to believe, for inching about on steep gradients with heavy weights seems an ideal situation for the torque-converter vehicle. But once again it's the practical experience of knowing how this Maxidyne engine can perform which has totally turned round the initial theorising. In fact, although this Bulldog does not have a very loud bark, Millers will tell you from experience it can have quite a bite.

The Mack, just like the HHTs, certainly looks the part as a heavy-haulage tractor but, if ever there were a competition for the most 'wolf-like' machine

under the most 'sheep-like' skin then FAJ299V must come close to winning. It is also quite a rarity in this select club for even though the Iveco Corporation has a large following for their trucks throughout the world, the name Fiat is not a regular sight in ultra-heavy haulage. FAJ has quietly graced the fleet of Econofreight for the last four years and even now still manages to look fairly innocuous. It is a standard looking 6 × 4 tractor and surely that plate with a manufacturers rating of 180 tons gtw must be a mistake? However, before we tear the vehicle to pieces let's just check its pedigree.

Its conception was the work of one Albin Von Bogert. Best described as an entrepreneur, one of Albin's interests was in VBA Trucking of Antwerp which, amongst other things, had the local Fiat dealership. When a heavy-haulage outfit was required for the fleet it seemed common sense to have two tractors of that make but Albin's specifications were so detailed that the factory was obliged to appoint Catrabel NVSA, also of Antwerp, to do the conversion work. The underlying trend in the modifications was strength. The chassis, the fifth wheel subframe, the rear axle casings, the wheels and even the propshaft were specially treated to meet the testing demands of the heavy-haulage business. Double compressors were fitted on the braking system to provide a better supply of air and the electrics were boosted to ensure adequate lighting on the lengthened outfit. An engine time clock was also fitted so that servicing could be geared to how long it had been working rather than to the mileage covered. The heart of the machine was the Fiat 8210.2 engine

The Fiat has Econofreight on the door, but its Nicolas configuration is virtually identical to that used by Albin Von Bogert, who had the machine built for his assorted fleet in Antwerp. The load was one of the 39 Farmer vessels moved to Hartlepool docks in the summer of 1982.

producing 300 bhp and driving through a 13-speed Fuller 9513 gearbox. The back bogie was a Fiat hub reduction and, although the low ratio does allow a gradability of 1 in 6 at 150 tonnes gtw, the top speed was cut to 38 mph.

The Fiats went to work but when Albin decided to sell up his haulage company and convert the premises into a sports centre, there were only 80 hours on the engine time clock which gave some indication of how little the machines had worked. Tom Llewellyn paid the depot a visit to purchase some Nicolas running gear but showed no interest in the 6 × 4 tractor parked in the corner, its sister having been burned out in a mysterious fire. It was only when Tom's number two, Roy Brandley, came over to collect the axles and utilised the Fiat to haul them down to Zeebrugge that the machine was able to show its potential. Roy has been brought up mating and driving heavy-haulage trucks and it was through the seat of his pants that he knew he had stumbled on quite a tractor. It was difficult to put his finger on the precise reason for his opinion but everything in the transmission line just clicked precisely into position. Even with the superlatives flowing from the Brandley tongue, Tom could not get too excited about the machine but eventually for the exchange of £17,000 the tractor was brought into the Econofreight fold. Four years later on, Mr Llewellyn concedes that deal was, perhaps, one of the best he has ever struck, for the 300PT has paid for itself time and again.

The regular driver is John Angles who feels that this tractor is perhaps the best machine in its class he has encountered and all he says is that the facts speak for themselves. Carrying 120 tons of concrete beam from Tallington to the new M56 in Lancashire, John was routed over the M62 and got to Hartshead services for the night. Next morning the police formed a convoy of three identical beams heading west so that traffic disruption was kept to a minimum. The Fiat was leading, Malcolm Johnson in Sunters' Titan II came next with a Sommerscales outfit at the rear. All ran together until the infamous Windy Hill was reached, which is a steep climb even for a 38 tonnes gross outfit but at nearly five times that weight it is a real test of strength. John put the Fiat into first, one above crawler, put his foot down and went for the top. No change of gear up or down was necessary as the tractor pulled well without flickering, in fact it pulled so well that at the summit the police stopped John so that Malcolm could catch him up as he had been left so far behind. The Sunter men were a trifle upset at the performance from the Italian job and on site their pride was dented even more. Having to haul the beam over a testing bailey bridge had not been achieved by any other 6 × 4

tractor without a double head, but John gave the Fiat a go and only just made it. He would not have done if one of the Sunter men had got his way for, thinking this upstart was performing far too well, he had mischievously tried to knock on the trailer deadman brake at the critical part of the climb over the hump-back bridge. Malcolm followed with the 420 bhp Titan in 6 × 4 drive but he had to admit defeat, back up, then lock up his 6 × 6 configuration before he could surmount the obstacle. The Fiat had shown its prowess.

John concedes that the machine is not perfect. The old-fashioned cab is noisy and when he is running with 20 tons of temporary ballast on his back, the wagon vibrates like mad. A torque converter may have enhanced the vehicle's performance but even as it stands the 300PT has proved to be full of surprises. John had 97 tons of machine on his Nicolas semi-trailer, the third of three identical loads which were hauled from Immingham to Whitehaven. Leaving Penrith on the A66 westbound, the previous loads pulled by Heanors and Brackmills had travelled the wrong way down the dual carriageway. This new stretch of road had flattened out the severe climb just beside the Stainton Village turn-off and gave the outfits the chance of doing the haul without a double head. John was told about this by the escorting police officer but felt the Fiat, even at 150 tons gross, could do it on the correct side of the dual carriageway and gave it a go. On dropping down into crawler, the lowest of all his gears, John recalls that the strangest thing happened. At the steepest part of the climb the engine went very quiet as the rev counter dropped and dropped. Trailerman Dave Walker had jumped out so that if the tractor faltered he could bang on the trailer deadman brake and even he thought the outfit had stopped for he was just standing still. Yet, in fact, the vehicle continued to inch forwards with the throttle on the floorboards and the engine only just above tick-over. All were surprised, and naturally relieved, as the gradient eased with the Fiat still going forwards. In hindsight it may have been better to have closed down the other carriageway to allow the outfit through, but Mr Angles was still very pleased that his prediction and faith in his mount had not been proven wrong. It only goes to prove that, if you do your homework correctly, then the strangest form of machine can prove to be a great asset in the heavy-haulage business.

If one heard that when John Wynn was moving mountains in distant Sudan he had used a local tipper loaded with ballast as his locomotive then although feeling it was rather incredible, one would naturally accept it as being one of the improvisations that the outback produces. But being told that two particular tractors of two separate UK hauliers based on Teeside, both in general national use, are in fact converted tippers seems just too much to swallow. This, however, is exactly the case of 145 Scania, registration JPY958W, and N10 Volvo RDC955X, although their appearance now bears no resemblance to their initial operating guise.

The Scania was built to meet the demands for dumpers in Northern Ireland but, being the last of a batch, it stood unused for some considerable time in the province before a prospective purchaser came along. Maurice Dawson of AV Dawson Ltd was not looking for a tipper but Geoff Colls from Union Trucks of Darlington assured him that the 6 × 4 chassis at 10¼-tons unladen would make an ideal heavy-haulage tractor for his assorted fleet. It seems a long way to go just for a test drive but the 145 gave a very good account of itself and, as the price was right, the deal was clinched. One thing that was not brought over the water was the dumper body which, at the time of writing, is still taking up space in that far-off dealer's yard.

The other sturdy Swede started life as a demonstrator for its makers in its home country fitted with a typical scow-ended dumper truck body over its deep, strengthened chassis. Going through its paces for prospective purchasers at Halarad one day, it struck Tom Llewellyn, who was on a busman's holiday, as being just the ideal machine he had in mind to fill a particular rôle in his fleet. He has no intentions of it carrying 20 tons of spoil around Teeside but, with the same amount of ballast on its back, it seemed ideal for hauling loads of over the magic 100 tons. Oddly enough Volvo did not offer the N10 as a heavy-haulage tractor in a specification which suited Tom, so when this particular chassis came up for disposal, Econofreight were quickly in to take it off their hands. Second-hand seems rather a harsh description when you consider that the Volvo had only done just over 5,000 kilometres; but on its first run it did not exactly create a lot of confidence

The outfit looked immaculate as it left the yard bound for Lancashire to pick up its first load. Driver Ernie Pickersgill had no trouble with the eight-speed gearbox plus torque converter and he was full of admiration for the sleeper cab added on by Riverside Motors of Selby, in fact it was more like working at the Ritz than being inside a lorry. The smooth-running empty Nicolas trailer followed easily behind but as Ormesby bank approached a strange thing happened to the outfit — it just did not want to go up. Ernie went down and down the gears and it took the lowest gear of all to surmount the incline. If that was what the vehicle was like when it was unladen, what would happen with 100 tons of payload on its back? The worries were

quickly dispelled for this unusual lack of power was only because the vehicle had been standing around for about a year and was virtually brand new and thus had to be run in. Two years later Ernie reports that as every day passes the tipper is pulling better and better, the ballast box may creak and groan a little as though it was shouting 'enough' but rarely will the machine submit when the question is asked of it.

This was notably demonstrated when the Port of London wanted one of their monster dockside cranes moved. True, the crane could move by itself but with its three axle loadings reading close to 100 tons each, it required a specially strengthened road to move about on. Getting it the three miles round the docks meant a trip aboard ten rows of extra wide Nicolas axles headed up by the tipper. To ease passage over a bridge one of the ex-Magnaload F89s was double headed but, in the main, the N10 did it alone with an all-up weight just on the 400-ton mark. The move naturally created a lot of interest with the dockers but the sheer structure of the massive crane was an awe inspiring sight making all would-be watchers keep well away fearing it would just topple over. However, as the haul went on, the easy ride gave the spectators more and more confidence to get closer and some even clambered up the ladders intent on watching the bubble. Fitted in the crane cab this device works like a spirit level ensuring the operator knows exactly how he stands. Steve Ford and the rest of the trailer crew had their own level but it was still very pleasing to be told that the ride given on the back of the Nicolas was actually more level than when the crane operated under its own power.

That was a particularly memorable one-off job, but it was at Mossmorran in Scotland that the tipper really showed its worth time and again. With Esso-chem Olefins constructing a new ethylene plant in this remote part of Fife, a great deal of abnormal-load traffic had to be hauled on to site. The nearest suitable seaport was at the Royal Naval base of Rosyth but the Scottish terrain really made it hard work to cover those 11 miles to site. The largest load moved by the N10 was an Air Products cold-box, the largest of its kind ever made, with vital dimensions of 130 ft long, 20 ft wide, 25 ft high, weighing in at 217 tonnes. It took nine hours to do the haul but, even though the Volvo did need occasional double heading, with a performance like this up your sleeve it is strange that the business is not flooded out with converted tippers. The key to its impressive performance is obviously the torque converter, but what exactly is this magical addition to the transmission and why does it make so much difference?

HHT001 is one special tractor but it was Heanor's Titanic trailer which made is possible to do this internal move at BSC Scunthorpe mid-1983. At 75 tons this Coke oven pushing machine would have struck the pipe gantry if carried on a standard modular trailer but the Searson formula applied to King and Cometto bits meant all of four ins clearance for this 26 ft high, 36 ft wide load.

003 pulls with 001 pushing 14 axles of Cometto trailer as the Heanor outfit leaves GEC Stafford in April 1981, with a 169-tonnes transformer. Destined for Poolberg in Southern Ireland, the load trekked up to Manchester docks at an all-up weight close to 300 tons.

Left and top right HHT002 was bought by Geoff Johnson of Barton but as well as moving 100-ton 'cracker' columns it was also expected to do rather mundane work like crawler cranes. It is using the six-axle Nicolas when seen in early 1983 passing through Forres en route to Ardeseir whilst the NCK machine is being moved locally at Redcar on a trailer Geoff had built himself.

Right and below right Millers well turned-out Mack-Cometto-Volvo road train is pictured on one of its many transpennine crossings, close to Delph on the A62. The 'Snow!' board had particular significance, for one of these 150-ton Markham taps was literally 'lost' for five days in a horrendous snow storm which even stopped 'Bonzo Bear'.

Left and below left Once the Mack reached Dinorwic, it was expected to inch its loads into the far extremities of the mountain with all the problems this incurred, ghosts included! The Markham tap has been eased 7/10th of a mile into the mountain, round acute corners and down 1-in-10 gradients as it approaches its final resting place.

Left 'Bonzo Bear' tends to grab lots of attention wherever it goes but when it moved this 'Puffing Billy' from Worth Valley to Leyland in about 1981 it was the load and not the tractor that the sightseers watched.

The Mack pushes out one of four 75 ft long, 25-ton columns made by Adamson and Hatchett of Dunkinfield for BP Kinneil near Grangemouth. Their carriage was particularly difficult, not so much because of the 15 ft 7 ins width, but because their physical make-up made it nearly impossible to position the rearmost bogie.

John Angles waits for the traffic to be halted before he sets the Fiat under way up this steep hill in Bristol. The 70-ton, 22 ft high crane-pedestal load was built by Stothert & Pitt and was designed to perch on the top of one of the North Sea oil rigs.

Awaiting the arrival of their police escort, the Mack-Cometto outfit is seen on the premises of Hawker Siddeleys at Walthamstow in mid-1983. Millers modified their girder-trailer to take the extra width of the 130-ton transformer which was eventually destined for Hong Kong. 'Bonzo Bear' only went as far as Tilbury but 30 miles in five hours was good time-keeping for the lengthy outfit.

Above The Fiat in ballasted-tractor form is leaving BOC Cryoplants at Edmonton with this box bound for Tilbury. Not a great deal of weight but at 104 ft long, the haulier used a four-bed-six Nicolas trailer for maximum stability and control.

Left and below left A.V. Dawson of Middlesbrough operate JPY958W, a Scania-Nicolas heavy-haulage artic, although the 145 was originally built as a dumper for Northern Ireland. Two of the many locomotives it has hauled include 92134, which is being manoeuvred at North Yorkshire Moor Railways Pickering terminal having been saved from the Barry graveyard for preservation, and the BSC shunter, which was hauled from Lackenby to Ravenscraig and is pictured going up Galley bank on the A66, all-up weight being 125 tons.

Opposite page Econofreight's 'tipper' is seen at London where it hauled this PLA 300-ton mobile crane a distance of three miles round the docks. It was double-headed for a short distance but at 400 tons gross it does show you what a torque converter can do to enhance a vehicle's performance.

This page and above right It was at Mossmorran that the N10 really showed its potential, hauling all sorts of loads on to site from the naval dockyard at Rosyth. Biggest of these was a very impressive Air Products cold-box whose vital dimensions were 130 ft long, 20 ft wide, 25 ft high and 217 tonnes in weight.

Right There was only 80 tons of weight in this unladen water-storage tank that the N10 moved in early 1983 on site at Seal Sands, but to ensure the best support the Nicolas load carrier was actually two ten-axled trailers joined side by side, which configuration is termed as 'four-file wide'.

11. Talk converted

In the late 1950s the Self-Changing Gears semi-automatic gearbox was being adopted in many of the heavy-haulage tractors then in use. Coupled to a fluid flywheel it meant that oil instead of clutch plates would transmit power from the engine to the gearbox thus resulting in the ability of the transmission to withstand heavier loadings and, at times, greater abuse from the driver. However, one of the drawbacks of this system is that the torque, or turning force output, is directly related to the torque input. In other words with no clutch pedal for the driver to slip as he endeavoured to ease the power in, it meant that the engine had to be working fast enough to spin the oil flywheel at the desired rate. Sometimes, however, this just was not possible.

An example of this disadvantage could be seen when Bill Jamieson was hauling the first of two massive package boilers from their manufacturers, Foster Whellers of Hartlepool, to the ICI chemical complex at Billingham in early 1983. Such were the limitations of the works' internal installations that the load had to be carried by means of end suspension to keep its height as low as possible, the framework being supported on two Nicolas bogies. The first eight miles were covered without incident but when turning sharp left on to Billingham bank things started to get very tricky. A combination of a tight turn with a very long, high load, manoeuvring past lamposts which should have been removed, found Bill and his Contractor reduced to a trickling speed. The bank had a gradient of just under 10 per cent but, even with his foot flat to the boards and first gear engaged, the combination of weight and incline just would not let the engine rev fast enough to propel the vehicle forwards. Bill could have reversed back across the junction and would have surmounted the bank with a run from the level but even with a police escort, this manoeuvre would have created traffic chaos. What the crew did to resume forward progress just goes to illustrate how odd this type of transmission can be.

All the Contractor needed in order to allow the Cummins engine to build up its speed and produce more power was for something or someone just to take the strain for a split second. A double head was the obvious answer but with no time to wait in getting anything bigger, what was coupled up to the front was a standard British Leyland Landrover. It is hard to believe but with that pulling at an all-up gross train weight in excess of 200 tons, forward movement was recommenced and the Scammell was able to clear the bank and deliver its load. Bill has had his leg pulled about this on several occasions and the local Landrover dealer may have been tempted to use the information in his sales chat, for technically speaking that Landrover did pull over 200 tons up that hill.

One way of ensuring more power is produced at very low engine revs is to utilise a torque converter. This addition to the transmission line has only in recent years been generally utilised in heavy-haulage tractors, although the concept is an old established engineering principle. It, too, utilises oil similarly to a fluid coupling, but with the insertion of an internal stator, with impeller and turbine, the amount of output torque that is produced can now be a vast multiplication of the input torque. What this means in practice is that even at just over tick-over speeds, heavy-haulage tractors can now produce the power and capability to be able to inch loads about in situations which normally would have warranted a great deal of slipping from the normal plate type of clutch.

George Curtis was made aware of this old principle when he was looking for a big tractor to add to his fleet of Transport Services (Lindsey) Ltd in the mid-1970s. Their F89, HEE313N, had been a very impressive performer but getting it slowly to manoeuvre 150-ton loads around Charlton Leslie's Wallsend yard underlined that this was asking far too much from it. Bigger load movements in the oil-rig yards were in the offing so a stronger new tractor seemed a natural progression to make. Mack had TSL interested in an Interstater fitted with an Allison automatic gearbox but, as Volvo were already established in the Lincolnshire fleet, they were asked if they could produce a 240-ton gross tractor. This sort of rating was unknown for any UK Volvo but, when George heard from an associate who had been in Australia driving the N12, he thought this version would do the trick. With the prospect of Mack hovering in the background to snap up the deal, the spur was given to Volvo to produce what was required and the order went to Sweden. The only thing which stumped them was that TSL's engineer, Peter Houghton, had insisted that a torque converter must be on the tractor's specification.

It took a whole year for PBE867S to appear for, as it was the first UK heavy-haulage Volvo fitted with a torque converter, its manufacturers had a great deal of development work to do on it before they were satisfied with its performance. It arrived just before Christmas 1977 with an eight-speed gearbox, although this was immediately replaced with a 16-speed version. Having gone down to Southampton for a sleeper cab, the bonneted tractor was soon put to the test in delivering three 165-ton Davey United castings from Sheffield to Immingham. On the first haul the ability of driver Mick Crawshaw was naturally questioned when the outfit turned into Monks Road, Lincoln, for progress stopped rather abruptly when an internal shaft in the gearbox snapped. Later examination showed this to be due to a faulty part but, by working through the night, the local dealer had the N12 operational by next morning. But what happened with the second load as it was en route from Sheffield was virtually an action replay as suddenly the propshaft snapped. Mick knew there was nothing wrong with his driving. George Curtis started to yell for a specially strengthened propshaft. But it was Stan Gilbert who came up with the reason for this failure and the solution preventing its recurrence. Looking at the tractor through an engineer's eyes, he noticed that the exhaust system passed very close to one of the joints of the lengthy propeller shaft. It seemed to him that the excessive heat created when the vehicle was working hard, was burning out the lubricating grease from the shaft's roller bearings. Using no grease at all would obviously prompt premature failure so a protective fire guard was fitted around the joint and thus the gremlins of the Davy Castings were defeated.

Running at an all-up weight of 249 tons on this cross-country haul seems quite impressive for the N12 but it was to be in site work where the torque converter was to show its worth. At 250 tons a time

the oil-rig leg sections moved at the Highland Fabricators Nigg Bay yard were not too excessive but their 'threepenny bit' top-heavy shape made the TSL crew appreciate the smooth control given by the sophisticated transmission. The extra-long wheelbase of the tractor also seemed to give greater stability for this type of job but when TSL tried to repeat their order for a similar vehicle Volvo were not interested. They were keen to supply an F12 with a similar specification as this was the model they were promoting in the UK, so the company bought WEE512V into the fleet. These two tractors working together were to give TSL a new strength which was ably demonstrated when they were involved in the movement of a massive Whessoe module on Teesside.

Initially two Contractors headed up the Volvos but the differing transmissions in the quartet were not conducive to satisfactory progress, so the Scammells were unhitched and the two Swedes left to do it themselves. 2,000 tons is heavy in anyone's book but this duo had enough strength between them to move this weight out of the preparation bay and on to the quayside prior to it being winched out to the waiting barge. TSL well liked this type of Volvo tractor so when Brackmill's similar BVV 26T came up for sale they had no hesitation in purchasing it. Its custom-built sleeper cab was worthy of inspection, although no one was surprised when they lifted the bunk to see an assortment of propshafts which had suffered from the gremlins. This minor defect apart, Volvos new heavy-haulage tractors are performing very well, as is a machine which shares its name with a famous Leyland bus.

Readers of Greek mythology are well aware that the Titans were a race of giants and, although Peter Sunter was not really into reading the classics, his globe-trotting heavy-haulage travels had meant he was fully acquainted with the name. Not a man to worry about being the first at doing something, it was still quite a big step when VVN910S came to enhance the Northallerton fleet. It may have been the first Titan to come into the UK, but Titan GmbH was a well established, special vehicle maker producing machines to order mainly based on Mercedes Benz parts from their fairly small premises at Appenweier, West Germany. In the main their heavy-haulage tractors were of 6×6 configuration but, having no real need for a driven front axle, Sunters specification was for a 6×4 unit which could be used either as an artic or as a ballasted tractor. The heart of the vehicle was the massive 21-litre Mercedes engine, unturbocharged but still pushing out 420 bhp. Driving through an eight-speed gearbox, plus WSK torque converter, meant that all and sundry were very impressed

Constables Baker, Smith, Slater and Longstaff of Clevelands 'chips' department were needed to escort this handful sitting on the back of the Titan's Nicolas semi-trailer. Late 1978 was the date when this vessel was hauled from Middlesbrough docks down to ICI Wilton.

except, perhaps, chauffeur number one, Ken Bickerton.

Having at the time only been 13 years at Sunters, Ken would be thought of as quite a youngster to take over the most powerful vehicle in the fleet but for the first load Ken did not let his heart rule his head and had the Titan under the microscope. He had regularly hauled the 65-ton BNFL flasks from Darlington to Carlisle with his 14-litre Scania so as man and machine left for Scotch Corner, he was conducting his own road test. Of all the Pennine crossings, the A66, especially with later modifications, is relatively pleasant but in 1977 Galley bank was a notable exception and could be quite a half-shaft snapper. With his previous Scania he had romped up here in second gear but for the Titan with the same type of load he was down into first. True, the vehicle was still tight but surely for an engine 50 per cent bigger it should do better than that? More disconcerting was an awful vibration which definitely should not have been there even if this was a new vehicle. So, with no more ado, the Titan was sent back to Germany for inspection. Being more used to producing 6 × 6s, the factory had, in fact, installed the transmission incorrectly. The angle which the propshaft took as it left the gearbox was too acute, thus bringing out a tremor in the vehicle. By canting the engine at a slightly different angle the distortion was removed and the machine was now vibration-free, although its reported lack of power could not be diagnosed as anything specific.

Back in the UK Sunters felt that, if Ken was right about the vibration, he may well be right about the power loss so, rather than have the vehicle fail whilst on the job, a sufficiently hard test run had to be organised. Ken and Charles Tomkins went out by

car to look for a route as not every county council was happy about 150 tons just joy riding around the area. Their travels took them up to Tyneside. 'What about Whickham Bank?', Ken suggested, 'that should be a good test for it.' 'Do you think it'll get up,' said Charles, 'it's a bit steep.' 'Of course it'll get up,' Ken responded, thinking to himself, 'It's like a house end that bank, it'll never get up there in a month of Sundays so they'll have to fit a couple of turbochargers to boost my power.' The bank was surveyed, Charles making his calculations and reporting it was 1 in 6 but marginally steeper in places. He reflected that 20 years earlier Wynns had hauled an 80-ton stator up this bank from Stella West power-station and at that time four assorted tractors were needed to clear the incline. Using only one machine with more weight on the same bank seems impossible but if Ken says it'll do it he must be right.

Back at base the paperwork was completed, the Titan's Nicolas semi-trailer loaded up and Ken headed north with over 100 tons of ballast on his back. Whickham bank was reached and down the box Ken went until crawler bottom was reached. The engine revs started to drop away but at 1,500 rpm, the torque converter cut itself in. It sounded as though the clutch was slipping Ken reported, but instead of coming to a juddering halt in a haze of asbestos smoke the Titan just kept going and going right to the top. The rest of the haul was an anti-climax and returning to Northallerton it was Ken and not the Titan who had to admit defeat.

Five years on Titan and Bickerton are still in combination. Their travels have taken paper-machine drums to Southern Italy and hauled enormous pipe-jacks and modules at the Shetlands' Sullom Voe. No complaints now about the slow plodding Titan although, with a top speed of only 42 mph, it means that crossing France takes five days. It does not help either that the outfit is banned from their motorways not because of its weight but because at 3 metres wide the trailer cannot get through the gap at the toll booths. Unaccompanied European heavy haulage is undertaken with peace of mind because Ken knows he has never had to have a double head out of trouble, although the Titan has regularly rescued others, not least of which is Watkinsons splendid Scania. Running down to Goodwood with loads of concrete, the duo were in convoy and on three occasions a snatch was wanted as the ballasted 'Ymir' could not get any grip. Twice Ken just hooked him on the end of his semi-trailer but on the third occasion he had to drop the trailer to go back and help. There was no ballast and no imposed load on the Titan but still enough power to help the stricken 146 forwards.

Helping out is all part of heavy-haulage life but when Keith Watkinson later came out to relief drive his ex-Sparrows Scammell Contractor a little bit of pride was at stake. 'You won't have to pull me with this,' he shouted at Ken as they both left Penrith on the A66 westbound again with concrete beams, but as Windscale got ever closer Keith was forced to eat his words. A slight blockage in the filters prompted fuel starvation for the big Cummins less than half a mile away from the site but on a testing incline. This gave no trouble to the Titan or torque converter which once again showed its true value for money.

The vehicle's self-reliability was ably demonstrated as Ken was taking one of four 100 ft long, 166-ton vessels from Hull round to Spurn Point using two six-row Nicolas bogies. It was not a very steep hill but the greasy road surface would not give the grip and the spinning drive wheels brought the outfit to a halt. Malcolm Johnson and Jack Higgins were following in Titan II but they could only stop and watch as Bickerton worked it out. Engaging the diff lock forced the drive axles tight, select first gear, clutch out, brakes off and with the convertor working hard the Titan inched away forwards at over 220 tons gross. The admiring observers could only reflect on how the fleet's Mk I Contractors would have done in such a situation. Theorising on how his Titan could be improved, Ken suggests two more gears in the gearbox, one very low one and one very high one, the latter, of course, for empty homeward-bound running. He sees himself at the wheel of a new Titan 8 × 8 and with 500 or even 600 hp under his right foot he could then really be considered a member of a gigantic race.

Offering not that much power but a similar transmission to the Titan were the big six-wheelers manufactured by fellow West Germans, Maschinenfabrick Augsburg-Nurnberg, known thankfully by their abbreviated title of MAN. British Nuclear Fuels were to buy one of their big Jumbos, BSM923X, when TSM65H and 66H, the two previously used lightweight Contractors, came up for replacement. Running between Chapelcross in southern Scotland and Windscale, Cumbria, the new 'coffin carrier' ran at virtually the same weight whether it was laden or empty. The 6 × 4 tractor weighed in at 11 tons empty, although 15 tons of lead ballast was permanently attached to its back. Its V10 engine, with characteristic raspish exhaust note, propelled the Crane Fruehauf four-axle drawbar trailer along. The 400 bhp developed at 2,500 rpm was more than enough power for the outfit as the regular all-up weight was only 94 tons, but there was always the performance of the torque converter to fall back on should the Lake District terrain dictate it.

Pickfords Heavy Haulage had been using the MANs long before the new, blue, nuclear-fuel carrier arrived in the form of machines like UYT585S, rated at 150 tons gtw and based at their Leicester branch. The Midlands depots preferred to use the MANs in articulated form with six or even seven axled semi-trailers so that their full rating could be fully utilised. The only drawback with this operation was the hefty complete unladen weight of the outfit which resulted in the bill for a 12 months' excise licence being close to £5,000, owing to the way taxation was calculated. Five years later, whilst inflation has increased the price of virtually everything, one may be interested to know that a similar annual tax disc for the same vehicle, doing the same heavy haulage work, up to the same 150 tons gtw, will now cost £170. Pickfords are not complaining about saving £4,830 on each of these vehicles per year. The early MANs, especially the smaller ones, were not without their mechanical problems although Pickfords found that the last two big ones they were to purchase proved a far better buy. CYL509V was coupled up to a similar Nicolas six-axled semi-trailer to that which Wynns' 'Renown' was hauling, whilst CYL510V, rated at 180 tons gtw, found itself as a ballasted tractor, pitched in to a very impressive move.

The weather in January for most of the UK is mostly inclement, although in Scotland it is normally worse, so when Scotts Shipbuilding of Greenock were required to do a refit on a 350-ton boat which would not wait for the arrival of finer days, to ensure maximum efficiency they decided the vessel should be moved indoors. It sounds all right if you say it quickly but with other dimensions being 100 ft long, 38 ft wide and 18 ft 6 ins high, it was not a dinghy which could be simply craned into position — so Pickfords were asked to do the job.

The first problem was getting the vessel out of the water, which was solved by following the Bradwell principle. A specially designed cradle was placed in the Clyde at the foot of a 1 in 25 building berth and, as the high tide swallowed it up, a tug manoeuvred the boat above the cradle which was clearly indicated by vertical guide posts. As the tide went back the boat settled on to the cradle which itself was resting in a wheeled trackway. The new MAN then came on to the scene and, assisted by another unit, it winched the cradle and boat a total of 400 ft up on to the drier dockside. Four power-operated jacks lifted the mass 4 ft off the ground which allowed a specially rigged 67-ton, 14-row Nicolas trailer to slip underneath. Even lowering it down on to the 88 ft long, 12 ft 3 ins wide load carrier was quite tricky and required the insertion of special beams to ensure weight distribution was correct. The pull across the shipyard and the push into the refitting shop was no long motorway haul, but with an all-up combination weight close to 500 tons, moved over a thick covering of slush and snow, the MAN and its transmission received an early baptism into the testing demands of ultra-heavy haulage.

The new Jumbo performed pleasingly well but the other tractor on the job, XUU919T, totally eclipsed the smaller MAN. It was definitely the bigger and more powerful vehicle and quite a a lot of people agreed that the Mk II version of the Contractor was the best heavy-haulage tractor ever to come out of Tolpitts Lane, Watford. Never a manufacturer to rush into anything hastily,

XUU925T is posed with one of the six loads that Pickfords Heavy Haulage moved into the Lindsey Oil Refinery at south Killingholme during August 1978. This column was 176 ft long, 12 ft wide and tipped the scales at 120 tons in weight.

Scammells did, however, realise that the advantages of the torque converter under certain heavy-haulage conditions were of considerable value to some potential customers. To bridge the gap between existing products and the entirely new range, the Mk II version of the Contractor was produced. This had not just a torque converter but a completely automatic transmission with the adoption of the Allison box so that all the driver needed to do was to pull the T-bar gear lever into the 2-5 notch and apply pressure through the right foot on to the two remaining pedals.

Along with this new gearing a new form of Cummins engine was installed, a 450 bhp KT unit, which ensured adequate compensation for the power loss created when using the automatic form of transmission. However, to live up to what its earlier Mk I sisters were capable of, ie, hauling weights three and four times their 240-ton gtw rating, Scammell added a four-speed Spicer auxiliary gearbox. The control for this was a simple round knurled knob and, prior to moving off, the driver just turned this to select a gear suitable to the weight he was pulling. Outwardly there was very little difference in the two models, although if you put them side by side the Mk II version is seen to be bigger and taller, breathing out even more strength and power. That impression was put to the test as 919T, along with identical XUU925T, became involved with all the big Pickford moves, especially the Davy casting.

It is probably natural to question why a 333-ton casting made in Germany for a steel-plate mill in Mexico comes to be trundling down the Doncaster motorway in the first week of January 1983, but this was the first of four similar loads en route from Dusseldorf to Sheffield where it was to be specially machined before crossing to America. Six months of preparation and planning had preceded that first haul which was full of interesting innovations.

By ship to Goole, the casting was then transferred

to a special canal barge, one form of transport which the Pickfords crew's ancestors had ample experience of using. The barge was able to reach Doncaster before the load had to be transferred on to the back of a Nicolas modular trailer. Doing both these lifts was a massive J. D. White's Demag TC4000 crane. With a capacity of 800 tons it was one of only two suitable cranes in the country which could do the job. It may have been the shortest part of the haul but reaching Sheffield was certainly the hardest. To appease certain highway authorities worried about weak stretches of road, Pickfords had to utilise 24 axles of running gear on their trailer. But even though all the 192 wheels could be steered independently, the roadtrain, headed up by the two big Scammells, was made less cumbersome by detaching four axles from the front and four from the rear of the Nicolas, as often as the engineers would allow. Even spreading the 533 tons all-up weight over a length of 213 ft, some bridges were still rather suspect and Brimsworth Road bridge had to be beefed up by affixing steel plates to the underneath with special glue developed by Sheffield University. However, one thing that did not lack strength in this tricky haul was the Mk II, which delivered the goods ahead of schedule and proved to Pickfords that sometimes biggest can be best.

Wynns Heavy Haulage of Stafford would certainly endorse this for in 'Superior', RWO73R, they have had six years' trouble-free experience in running the Mk II. This was joined by 'Invincible', DBO661V and eventually by DBF133Y and 134Y, the last and final two crew-cab Contractors to be built. The combining of Wynns with Wrekin Roadways now makes this operator the biggest user of the Contractor in the UK, although hitching anything smaller to their massive Cometto and Nicolas girder trailers would certainly look out of place.

Their Welsh predecessors started using the girder-trailer concept as far back as 1943, although 40 years on their latest versions can now offer nearly four times that original 90-ton capacity. Wynns were also one of the first users of the air-cushion equipment to spread the weight on their 12-axle trailers, but the present thinking at Stafford has taken yet another step forward. To save time and expense with the ACE gear the Wynns men now find themselves simply adding on more axles. Not in the same way that Pickfords did on the side of the M1, but if you have ever been waiting for a bus outside the GEC Stafford works you will know what I mean.

Because of the close confines of these works sometimes the 20-row girder trailers just cannot get in and out as desired, so Wynns' answer is to load up initially on the 14-row, run outside to the bus stop

One of the escorting police motor-cyclists, Malcolm Wilson, recorded this moment for posterity. A British Leyland Landrover is about to haul in excess of 200 tons up Billingham Bank although it was assisted by Bill Jamieson in his Scammell Contractor.

then simply rebuild the trailer to a 20-row. The weight is first taken off the load and main girders by building up with timbers and then the supporting necks and seven-row bogies are detached and pulled out of the way. Different necks on top of ten-row bogies are then pushed into place at either end, linked up and then the lifting of the load on its original girders makes the 300 tons plus of electrical equipment more bearable to the road surface on its journey out of Staffordshire. Wynns adopted this exchange idea just outside of Peterborough with a smaller load, because they found it better to haul the two separate ten-row bogies across country rather than utilise the sophisticated air blowers when a weak stretch of road had to be negotiated. Seeing these neck-combined axles pass by individually did strike one as rather odd as it seemed pretty obvious that there was something undoubtedly missing. I doubt, however, if Ron Savage or the rest of the Wynns drivers would like to be stopped and told he had lost his load plus half his trailer.

Wynns have certainly shown great faith in this big Scammell although plenty of others, including Pickfords, are quietly dropping them from their fleet. With many foreign competitors knocking at the door are the British manufacturers in a state to continue to fight in the market place? Can they show that buying British is best?

Left Tony McPartland of Reflecttions Studio, Yarm, was on hand to record this memorable occasion when the two Volvos pulled out 2,000 tons of Whessoe module prior to it being loaded out at Dock Point, Middlesbrough.

Left and below left Either line-ahead or side-by-side, this pair of torque-converter Volvos give TSL the ability to move some very impressive objects. In excess of 200 tons may not be particularly heavy but this load's high centre of gravity demanded very delicate carriage.

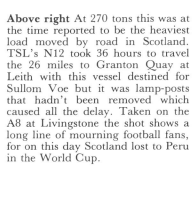

Above right At 270 tons this was at the time reported to be the heaviest load moved by road in Scotland. TSL's N12 took 36 hours to travel the 26 miles to Granton Quay at Leith with this vessel destined for Sullom Voe but it was lamp-posts that hadn't been removed which caused all the delay. Taken on the A8 at Livingstone the shot shows a long line of mourning football fans, for on this day Scotland lost to Peru in the World Cup.

Right It only went just down the road from BSC at Scunthorpe, but it was recorded that to allow the F12 and this package boiler through, 109 telegraph poles had to be lifted.

Above MGE180V started life with McKelvies but in early 1983 travelled south of the border to enter the Econofreight fold. Carried on the York trailer is one of three loads of 128 ft-long roof-trusses that were hauled from Thirsk to Barnard Castle.

Left One of the miracles of heavy haulage is how you move cranes like this in one piece. It's not the first time its been done nor will it be the last but the sight in William Press' yard at Haverton Hill can still take your breath away.

F12 BVV26T sported a torque converter and a very special sleeper cab. Brackmills worked it hard, coupled up to a Nicolas semi-trailer although when it passed on to TSL they used it in ballasted form right up to its 240 ton gtw rating.

There was only 49 tonnes in this paper drum but the haul down to Cuneo in Italy was one of the longest undertaken for the combination of Titan and driver Ken Bickerton. Both are seen backing onto the Normandy Ferries' ro-ro ship in the summer of 1982 prior to crossing the Channel.

Titan I is close to the end of a long haul from Yate near Bristol to Howden on Tyneside. Between Avonmouth and Wallsend the Mercedes 21-litre engine was very economical on its diesel fuel although it must be said that it was being carried on the back of the *Kingsnorth Fisher*.

Right Malcolm Johnson slips over Newport Bridge, Middlesbrough, with one of four 177-tonne vessels that were hauled in convoy from Thornaby to Hartlepool in the summer of 1982. It was to be a day that he wouldn't forget for a long time.

Right BSM923X was one of two MAN Jumbos bought by British Nuclear Fuels as a replacement for their 11-year-old Scammells. No change to the Crane Fruehauf drawbar trailers nor in the outfit's all-up weight of 94 tons for the regular bread run between Windscale and Chapelcross.

Right Yet another ICI module moved internally at their Wilton works in 1981 gives some indication of the dramatic advancement in heavy haulage that the hydraulic modular trailer has allowed. Sunters' Titan II is the workhorse on this occasion.

Opposite page Quite a line up of firepower as Wynns 'Invincible' joins three other torque-converter-fitted vehicles poised to haul yet another Whessoe mountain-type construction. The shot of the three Sunter vehicles in line ahead allows direct comparison between the sturdy Scammell and the 'tiny' Titan.

Above The Mark II Contractor is slightly bigger, taller and at 18 tons 15 cwt unladen, heavier than its early Mark I sister. XUU925T was one of a pair bought by Pickfords and is seen to be breathing out an aura of even more strength and power.

Right, top to bottom January 1983 found this impressive Pickford's roadtrain trundling down the motorway near Doncaster. If you count the number of axles you will see that eight lines have disappeared so that the handling of the 213 ft long outfit could be made slightly easier. The 333-ton casting had come from Germany and was en route to Sheffield for machining prior to export to Mexico.

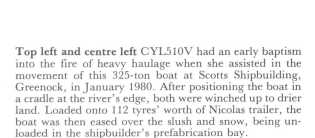

Top left and centre left CYL510V had an early baptism into the fire of heavy haulage when she assisted in the movement of this 325-ton boat at Scotts Shipbuilding, Greenock, in January 1980. After positioning the boat in a cradle at the river's edge, both were winched up to drier land. Loaded onto 112 tyres' worth of Nicolas trailer, the boat was then eased over the slush and snow, being unloaded in the shipbuilder's prefabrication bay.

Left CYL510V again heads up XUU919T as they are seen on the outskirts of Glasgow hauling a damaged 307-ton stator core from Inverkip power-station. Carrying all the weight is the 12-axle Crane Fruehauf girder-trailer, well into its second decade of hard use.

Left and below left Pickfords' dynamic duo are seen at UEI Methil in July 1982 with loads which are typical of what is moved round the oil-rig construction yards. In excess of 500 tons of steel is in each of these pieces but that is small when you consider that the finished skeleton of the rig weighed a massive 35,000 tons.

Bottom left 'Superior' was Wynns first Mk II Contractor, the company having high regard for the automatic transmission of this machine. November 23 1978 sees her slipping off the Starman boat at Tilbury docks with a Foster Wheeler load destined for Coryton.

Below 'Invincible', Wynns' second Mk II Contractor is also seen with a Foster Wheeler's load, having just performed a three-point turn at the junction of Church Street and Lynn Street in Hartlepool. I wonder how many people would pass their driving test if they had to perform that manoeuvre with this type of loaded combination.

Above right Gently does it. 'Superior', 'Challenger' and Nicolas axles ease this 40-ft diameter vessel on to site in March 1979. At 450 tonnes it was the largest of 21 loads moved by Wynns into the new Mobil extension being built at Coryton near Canvey Island.

Right The 1-in-6 Buttrells Hill never gets any easier to climb and four Contractors pushing out 1,570 bhp were required to haul this Wynns outfit up the incline as it made its way to Aberthaw power-station in April 1980.

Below right Making the front page of the Peterborough Evening Telegraph on 1st February 1983 was the Wynns –GEC contract outfit. Only 150 tons weight in this load which was hauled from Toddington to Walpole near Wisbech, but weak stretches of roadway dictated all 20 axles should be used under the girder-trailer to ensure that passage was as painless as possible.

12. The British fight back

The pedigree established by British manufacturers for producing heavy-haulage tractors goes without saying. Walk down Croft Street in Preston and you may be lucky enough to see a slice of their history taking up a fair amount of room in the haulage yard of Chris Millers. The WHG563V registration belies the fact that this Mk 3A Thornycroft Antar was manufactured way back in 1964, although when purchased by its present owners it was virtually in mint condition for a vehicle then 15 years old. It had, of course, only one previous owner who had not bothered to register this or any of its other vehicles in the normal fashion. Its rather drab paintwork was not usual nor was a canvas tilt directly behind the cab but, of course, all these things were normal to a vehicle of Her Majesty's Forces intended primarily as a battle-tank transporter.

Even in the middle 1980s the Antar still forms a big part of the Army heavy-haulage fleet although over the years during which they have been built it is strange that very few have slipped out to work in civvy street. Would-be operators may have been put off by page one of the War Office user handbook which describes the vehicle as a 50/60-ton tractor. For anyone who gives this a great deal of thought it seems ridiculous to buy a 10 ft 6 ins wide vehicle weighing in at over 21 tons empty which can only pull three times its own weight. However, fortunately for enthusiasts at least, Chris Miller was not put off by these minor details.

'Bonzo Bear' was working hard between Chesterfield and Dinorwic but the efficient way in which the Miller men were seen to be performing meant that extra work, especially on site in North Wales, was coming their way. The Mack could not be everywhere at once so it was obvious that another big tractor was required, preferably one based on the mountain. It was difficult to justify something brand new, but where do you buy a second-hand 200-ton tractor in the right condition at the right price? Miller's men went to Northern Ireland and down to the south coast in their search, although Chris ended up going to Priestbridge service station, Morpeth, Northumberland, the premises of GK Jackson & Son who had for sale one hardly used Thornycroft. A quick test ride down the A1 and back was all that he had to go on but the gut feeling that the vehicle promoted meant the sale was quickly transacted with both parties being very happy. Chris was especially pleased that he now had some strong back-up for his Mack and Volvo, which obviously made him more independent should anything untoward occur.

Back at base the Antar was stripped of its military shroud but, apart from a repaint and minor tow hitch modifications, there was very little to do to it before it was ready for heavy-haulage, Lancashire style. The machine had a natural air of sheer power about it, although the Preston men did wonder what they had bought. There was no fancy plate affixed to the vehicle by the manufacturer to say what the vehicle could haul and the user handbook made rather depressing reading. 'The vehicle is capable of operating with a trailer at gross train weights of $106\frac{1}{2}$ tons under favourable conditions,' it read, although favourable conditions for an Army vehicle could mean anything. The powerhouse of the machine was the mighty straight eight-cylinder Rolls Royce C8SFL supercharged engine. Its 16.2 litres produced 313 bhp at 2,100 rpm and 950 lb/ft of torque, so surely it could move more than 100 tons gross. The transmission was a bit odd, for the four-speed main gearbox and three-speed auxiliary were combined through one gear-lever to give only six forward gears and one reverse, although the 14.4 rear axle ratio meant that the overall ratio for bottom gear was 138.8 to 1. Read the fine print of the book and one is reassured to see that the maximum gradient which can be climbed whilst laden (at $106\frac{1}{2}$ tons gross) is given as 1 in 5.5, which to a heavy haulier is territory which certainly requires a double heading tractor. The answer to all the theory was, of course, to see what it could do in practice.

From Chesterfield to Huddersfield was a testing run for the Antar, even with the six-wheeled Volvo pushing, for at 150 tons the Markham taps bound for Dinorwic were the heaviest loads which Millers had moved. The Cometto girders and modular running gear brought the outfit's all-up weight to 265 tons — which is heavy by anyone's standards — but for Chris Miller it was the chance to see what the Antar could do. Being banished from the M62 because of their excessive weight, the heavy hauliers' route over the Pennines from Huddersfield is the testing A62 and Stanedge. Could this be described as 'favourable conditions'? It seemed difficult to think so but what was in Millers favour was that they had both the Mack and the 6 × 4 Volvo there on the scene. So with fingers crossed the Swede was unhooked and at 235 tons gross it was up to the Thornycroft and driver Mick Bradley to get to the top. The noise may have been a trifle on the loud side to all the pedestrians who were able to jog past it, but the 2½ miles were little problem to the Antar and it more than showed that its membership of the 100 club was displayed in practice if not on paper.

The three years since 1980 have seen the Antar back in the domain for which it was really built. Having the Thornycroft based at Dinorwic has meant that Millers could offer the service of a strong tractor for jobs which may not have been financially viable if a vehicle had to run down empty from Preston. Pulling over 200 tons gross on the road is relatively simple when you compare it to some of the jobs it did both on and inside the Elidir mountain. The rear 14.00 × 24 tyres are fairly soft at 50 psi and literally spread on the soft ground. Ample grip is afforded but even then Millers' men have had the Antar bouncing as it fought for grip whilst pulling low-loaders over peaks so severe that they have had to sledge over on their bottoms.

As the Dinorwic work eventually ended for Millers the Thornycroft came back to Lancashire. The Miller fleet may not be excessively large but it has gained one proven mountain mover that has worked inside and over the mountain.

Powerful though it may be the Antar was not everyone's cup of tea, but for those whose needs were not satisfied by the run-of-the-mill machine, there was always a small place in Cheshire which could be relied on to produce something special. For the last five decades Fodens of Sandbach have always been prepared to produce a tractor to a specification where the customer preferred to start with a clean sheet of paper. Fellow Sandbachians ERF were asked to do pretty much the same thing when Brian Rodwell approached them in the late

1970s for something which was not a regular production option.

Trading as Leicester Heavy Haulage of Loughborough, Brian's fleet is one of the few assorted haulage operations which is solidly ERF and that includes some rare four-wheeled platform general-haulage units. It's not that he was a great flag waver, it's just that he preferred to buy British when and if he thought the product was good enough. Progressing from an old Scammell to a Leyland Hippo, which used to haul all sorts of phenomenal weights, Brian standardised on ERF with models all the way up the scale to PRN648R which was rated for 120 tons gtw operation. But with loads of 100 tons plus starting to loom up, Brian and his dealer, Cossington Commercial Vehicles Ltd, went back to Sandbach for an even stronger tractor.

NUT345W took a long time to appear, although in hindsight the wait was well worthwhile. The heart of the tractor is the 14-litre Cummins NTE 350 engine, similar to that which is used in the Scammell Contractor, producing 335 bhp and 1,100 ft/lb torque. Transmitting the power to the Kirkstall axles carried on Hendrickson rubber suspension is a 20-speed Spicer gearbox (five selections in a high and low range, ten gears doubled up with a splitter). A Spicer twin-plate, ceramic-lined clutch is

The Thornycroft Antar certainly looks its part as a heavy-haulage tractor although Millers WHG563V is one of the very few 21-ton-unladen machines that have slipped out of the Army to work in 'civvy street'. June 10 1980 found it assisting 'Bonzo Bear' with one of two Morris Cranes that this company assembled on site at Dinorwic. There was only 70 tons in the load but a 1-in-6 gradient with a loose, greasy surface is not territory that you want to get stuck on and two is always better than one.

used which, after three years of hard work, was just about to be replaced, some reflection on the great pride and care taken by regular driver Don Moore. With rear axles rated at 18 tons each, the ERF can take heavy traffic when operating as an artic but it is frequently to be found in ballasted form running with eight rows of Cometto trailer. Prior to purchasing his modular trailers, Brian discovered that the Italian product was an inch and a half lower than anything else. Not a great deal to get excited about, but when Pickfords Glasgow-based MAN-Nicolas artic came down for a load at nearby Brush Electrical they could not get out the warehouse door because of their height. The ERF-Cometto has been regularly hauling out the same boxes, so the meagre inch and a half *did* make a difference.

The heaviest load hauled so far by the tractor is one of Brush's generators weighing in at 130 tons. The all-up weight would not be far away from 200 tons yet the journey over to Liverpool docks proved to be no great problem. More difficult was the carriage of a 58-ton, 85-foot long column which was made in Cardiff but had to be taken up to Manchester where it was internally coated with a special thick ceramic paint. Part of a desalination plant being constructed in Saudi Arabia, the vessel was then hauled across to Hull docks prior to the long sea journey south. To give the best support for the delicate load the two four-row Cometto bogies were linked with a lattice-type framework forming a 60-foot long trailer. Don Moore used extra thick rubber matting to make sure his securing chains did not do any external damage and the ballasted ERF pulled as smoothly as she could through the special 17-foot long drawbar on the cross-Pennine haul. A meticulous examination was still conducted at the docks but, even though the £2½ million of load was passed as all right, the Leicester men still had a week's wait while a Sparrows 54-foot long lifting beam was brought to the ship so that the vessel could be loaded correctly. Connecting this up to the ship's own loading winch the dockers swung it into position above the load and gently lifted it off the trailer. Don eased the ERF-Cometto forward out of the way just in time to witness the failure of the winch as the vessel reached its highest point. The wire rope ran free so that the column did not stop falling, via a bounce off the side of the ship, until it smashed into the quayside. Ouch! One glance inside at what was once a smooth pot-like interior revealed this now resembled a spider's web. Its return to the makers at Cardiff did not require such gentle transportation.

With a top speed of only 44 mph, it is rather sedate when compared to general haulage units but, like Econofreight's Fiat, the ERF is a powerhouse in disguise. When Don's vehicle is coupled up to a normal tandem-axle semi-trailer he is virtually indistinguishable from any other well turned out ERF six-wheeler, one thing which could never be said about the mountain movers which were built in Watford. From the very first, the sight of a Scammell on the road could never be confused with seeing anything else. The fact that the company merged with Leyland in 1955 made little difference to their characteristic appearance, although eagle-eyed observers would have noted that the main part of the cab on the lightweight Contractors bore a striking resemblance to the cab of the Leyland power-plus range adopted briefly in the early 1960s. This total independence was finally to be eroded in the late 1970s when Leyland introduced their long-awaited T45 range. The Crusaders were to disappear whilst the Leyland Octopus and Routeman eight-wheelers were to merge into the oddly named Leyland Constructors. But it was when Leyland produced their Landtrain as a replacement for the export Super Beaver and Hippos that Scammell saw this as just what they were after and their expertise revamped it to produce their bonneted S24 range as a replacement to the 20-year-old Contractor.

The concept of the S24 was to standardise on components throughout the range, with outwardly the same vehicle being rated between 50 and 300 tonnes gtw. Based on the 14-litre 'Big Cam' Cummins NTE 350 engine, turbocharged and aftercooled to produce 350 bhp and 1,100 lb/ft of torque, the difference in their capacity revolved round the rear axle ratios and the types of transmission adopted. The lightweights had the Allison automatic five-speed box, the middleweights the manual 15-speed Fuller whilst the strongest models had the 10-speed Spicer coupled to a Brockhouse torque converter. Scammell were no doubt pleased with their new offering although it was its image which would also affect their sales.

However, its image was enhanced when some very good promotion work came up with a particular brand of chocolate. 'Yorkie' had used the tough lorry driver image to emphasise how big and chunky their chocolate bars were. The early TV adverts used a big Mack but in later promotions of the same product the Mack was deleted and the big Scammell appeared in its place. The S24 had arrived. The early 1980s was a quiet period for some heavy hauliers but the S24 soon found its way on to the roads. Wards of Durham put to work KCU520X, a very impressive 125-tonner which demanded attention wherever it went.

Hauling heavier weights, was XTM546X, an early demonstrator, which first went to the Army for testing as a battle-tank transporter. It then did the rounds of several hauliers but, when it came to Mammoet-Econofreight, they would not let go of it and eventually purchased it. It showed its worth up at Mossmorran hauling numerous sorts of vessels to the new gas project under construction. However, it was back at home where its massive potential was ably demonstrated.

Ousting 'Betsy' as the fleet flagship, the S24 was naturally the first choice for all the big hauls, none of which was much bigger than the two massive coke drums which were built by Head Wrightsons of Thornaby and eventually destined for Lincolnshire. The dimensions of each drum were 26 ft 6 ins high, 22 ft 4 ins wide and 145 ft long, which is particularly problematic when you realise the left-hand turn out from their makers is a 180-degree manoeuvre. Supporting the load were ten rows of Nicolas axles, termed as three-file wide, which meant it was a trailer and a half, side by side, whilst a heavy Nicolas deck held the front and rear bogies together. This first turn was the hardest of the haul down to Middlesbrough docks for both driver Ernie Pickersgill and the S24, for as well as an all-up weight of 341 tons, a persistent light drizzle made the road surface very greasy. With the load using all the roadway Ernie had only inches to spare, far too tight a squeeze for one of the 120 tyres which went off with a bang as it ran over some ornamental footpath which looked more like a model of the Himalayas. With Ernie having slowly to manoeuvre backwards and forwards on an uphill ten-point turn, it

was the Brockhouse torque converter which ensured maximum control. The Cummins exhaust was a subdued murmur in comparison to the clang of the automatic radiator shutters opening and closing, but the smooth-running S24 amply demonstrated that it may well be smaller but it is no less impressive than the earlier Contractor.

Even smaller in stature was the S26 range which appeared identical to the Leyland Roadtrain general-haulage machine. The one big difference was that, unlike the standard T45 built for 38 tonnes gross operation, the Scammell version can be fit for 300 tonnes gtw. Like the S24, the Cummins NTE 350 is the standard engine with the Spicer 12-speed gearbox and Brockhouse torque converter taking the strain in the strongest models. Pickfords were quick to adopt the S26 as a replacement for their Jumbos in the 150-ton artics class, whilst Wynns were able to obtain the ballasted-tractor version as a demonstrator for some time. Both types are bringing favourable reports.

A lot of eyes will be focused on this particular range of Scammell as the 1980s progress. Some may comment that it has taken Watford a long time to produce a heavy-haulage tractor which is environmentally acceptable, as it does not actually look like a heavy-haulage machine. Be that as it may, the S26 appears to be the answer for many heavy hauliers. It may not have a strong sounding, old-fashioned name, but the future of the British heavy-haulage mountain movers is certainly being supported on its sturdy frame.

One of the many difficult jobs experienced by the Antar at Dinorwic was assisting in the haul of these winch drums up to the highest point on the Elidir mountain, 2,000 ft above sea level. 40 tons of load was pulled over humps so severe that the trailer had to sledge over on its bottom and the weather — for mid-June — was rarely very pleasant.

Left and below left Brian Rodwell's Leicester Heavy Haulage is one of the few general/heavy-haulage operators that is solidly ERF. Their current fleet flagship is NUT345W, a 6 × 4 unit rated by its manufacturers at 170 tonnes gtw. Shown on one of its early jobs it is taking a 96-ton stator set to Liverpool docks utilising eight rows of Cometto running gear.

Left Stewart and Maxwell Ward of Durham operate KCU520X, a very well turned-out S24, which was reportedly the first of its kind to operate in the UK. Currently only rated for 125 tons gtw, it normally carries the company's heavy plant machines on its Transquip trailer. However August 6 1983 saw its stability required to haul this 28 ton stone-crushing machine from Aycliffe to Allenheads.

Above An early demonstrator of the biggest of the S24 range, the 300-ton gtw model, found itself on trial by the Army as a potential tank transporter. They were later to favour the larger Scammell Commander. It's interesting to see that mudguards were not considered suitable to be fitted on this particular model. **Below** After the Army trial the vehicle received the registration of XTM546X and did the rounds of various hauliers. It ended up with Econofreight who worked it hard up at Mossmorran and is seen passing the Cottage Inn still sporting its original rather drab paintwork.

This page Econofreight were to eventually purchase XTM546X and although it did receive a brighter coat of paint there was no time for it to be off the road to have a ballast box fitted. Two of the many massive loads it hauled towards Mossmorran were this NEI boiler and an Air Products cold-box which is being eased back onto the *Aberthaw Fisher* on Merseyside.

Opposite and following page Head Wrightsons of Thornaby built two of these coke drums; the challenge to deliver them to Lincolnshire was accepted by Econofreight. All-up weight was 341 tons and at 145 ft long, 22 ft 4 ins wide, it is seen to be quite a handful for driver Ernie Pickersgill as it leaves the works in late June 1983. The extreme turn proved too much for one of the 120 tyres fitted to the Nicolas trailer which went off with a mighty bang as it ran over some ornamental footpath which looked more like a model of the Himalayas.

Right There was over 400 tons in this 125 ft wide launch truss that the S24 moved at RGC Methil in mid-1983. More pleasing to the Econofreight crew was being able to place this hefty construction within ⅛ ins of where it was wanted.

Right and below right Hills of Botley were to operate LTR689Y which was expected to do a lot of varied work. Particularly impressive was a 160 ft 9 ins long, 11 ft 6 ins wide, submarine cable gantry that they moved on March 13 1983. It only weighed 34 tons and was just moved down West quay road, but it did stop traffic for the day as it was lifted into position.

Overleaf The S26 is the latest offering from Scammell. Outwardly it looks no different from a six-wheeled Leyland Roadtrain but under its skin there is a great deal of power and strength waiting to be utilised. A great deal of eyes, both operators and other manufacturers, will be focussed on this particular range as the 1980s progress.